Cary Tennis

# Citizens
## of the
# Dream

*Advice on Writing,
Painting, Playing, Acting
and Being*

**CARY TENNIS BOOKS,** LLC
*San Francisco*

These columns first appeared on Salon.com

FIRST EDITION

Tennis, Cary,
Citizens of the Dream / Cary Tennis.

ISBN 978-0-9793270-4-9
1. Creativity. 2. Creative Ability.
I. Title
Printed in the United States of America
10 9 8 7 6 5 4 3 2 1

Book design by Norma Tennis

*For Pat Schneider, whose
Amherst Writers and Artists workshop method
greatly improved my creative life*

# Contents

INTRODUCTION ........................................................vii

A GENERAL THEORY OF CREATIVITY ...........................1
High highs, low lows ...............................................3
Can a former ugly duckling become
    a handsome leading man? .....................................7
I'm restless and creative but don't know where to begin ..........11
I'm dying to be a musician ......................................15
I don't feel like writing. Does that mean I'm not a writer?.......20
I'm afraid I'm doing the wrong art .............................23
Writing is in my blood, but how do I know
    if I'm any good? ..............................................29
Will our words ever be heard again?............................34
I peed at my desk in third grade and now I'm afraid to sing ....38

THE PERILS OF HIGHER EDUCATION ...........................45
What am I doing here?............................................47
Graduate schools can drive you crazy ..........................50
I got the writing fellowship—so now I'm terrified! ............54
I'm an art-school dropout wannabe!.............................58
I was fired for doing my job as a teacher ......................61

MAKING ART AND MAKING MONEY ............................65
I'm working for a cokehead at a free arts magazine.............67
I'm not afraid of writing, but I am afraid of publishing.........70
I need more ideas! Where do they come from? ..................75
How can I get a writing job?.....................................78
I'm an artist going crazy in a dysfunctional magazine!..........82
I'm doing stand-up and it's working. Should
    I quit my job? .................................................86
I'm a jazz pianist, nearly 50, and I need to make
    some real money! ............................................89

Entanglements, Obligations and
    the Soul of the Artist ................................95

My husband supported me in my art—
    should I now support him? ...............................97

Should I move to the city for my art? ......................100

My sister is a famous designer—and I'm not! .........................104

My husband shuts me down when I mention
    fine arts grad school...................................109

I live in a secret fantasy world................................ 114

Overcoming Distractions, Beating Blocks
    and Getting it Done....................................119

I get distracted by the Internet when I try to write .............121

The slush pile gave me writer's block!...................................126

Why am I obsessed with celebrity gossip?...........................132

I'm rewriting the same paragraph over and over and over!....137

Dear Sir, I write today to say that I cannot write...................145

I'm making progress in my art but feel like
    it's all a dead end ............................149

I'm an interesting, talented artist but I can't
    take the rejection! ........................... 154

Now that I've got my master's in writing...
    I'm not writing! ............................... 160

I'm an artist terrified of the vast, blank canvas....................164

Go away, can't you see I'm writing?! ......................168

Starting Over. Starting a Band. Just Not Giving Up...173

Is it too late to start a band at 45? ........................ 175

Midlife crisis: I could have been a singer! ..............179

At 56 I want an art history degree .........................183

I'm a singer—but I drift from waitress job to waitress job.....186

Should I give up on having a life in the theater?....................191

# Introduction

Dear Reader,

THIS IS A COLLECTION OF ADVICE COLUMNS I have
written for Salon.com between 2001 and 2011 on the subject of
living a creative life. The questions come from writers, painters,
musicians, singers, actors, standup artists and others. They ask
searing, personal yet universal questions such as how to overcome creative blocks, avoid distraction, find the best medium of
expression, make life changes to pursue an art, manage personal
relationships pinched by creative pursuits, reconcile the creative
and the social and so forth.

If you are familiar with my work for Salon.com you will know
that I do not just offer practical advice but attempt to make lyri-
cal leaps of the imagination and follow stray intrigues of thought
the same way that any other artist would. You may also know
that since 2007 I have been leading writing workshops using
the Amherst Writers and Artists method pioneered by poet and
teacher Pat Schneider. I dedicate this book to Pat because her
method has helped me in my writing more than any other single
thing save the reading of literature itself. It has helped me overcome certain stigmas of personality and recover from certain
wounds.

The idea behind the title *Citizens of the Dream* is that as creative people we live in our own country with its own physics and
history, its own atmospheres and rivers, its own maps. It is a
strange country but it is where we belong. It is our country. When
we try to live in "the real world" the way we think we're supposed to then we become unhappy. We do not know why we are
so unhappy living in the real world because we figure we ought to

be able to live in it just like other people. But we are different. We are citizens of the dream. And we might as well accept that we're different and set about establishing a way of living that meets our particular needs.

As creative people, we are workers of a special kind. We are producers but we do not produce beef or tires. Because we do not produce beef or tires our work is valued differently. When people are short on cash they continue to buy beef and tires but they do not buy poetry. Poetry they can get for free and we stand by full of fury but what can you do? People need their beef and they need their tires.

We all need money so when money does not come from our endeavors we panic. It seems as though the world is against us.

We need to be rewarded for our work but often what we need is not exactly money. More than others, we traffic in the currency of goodwill and esteem. We traffic in the currency of joy. Our balance sheet is tallied in happiness and wisdom. We take note of how much we have imparted and how much we have received.

If we are painters we place on our balance sheet how many enraptured viewers have stood before our paintings. Likewise with every medium and practitioner.

If we rely on money alone to indicate our work's value we may sink into despondency or, if our work is of the unusual kind that attracts great sums of money, then we may be led into error of a different kind. It is not that people value our work or do not value it. But they value it differently from beef and tires. They pay us in compliments, goodwill and other alternative currencies of the dream world.

This can make us angry and we say, Hey! Pay us in money! And if we can get money for our work, that is great. But it is also OK to accept how people receive our work, and to learn from how they respond to it. Let them do this. Let them decide what our work means to them. That is part of our gift: to observe. If we have to have a day job, that is OK. We don't own this thing called creativity. We are stewards; we cannot always expect it to pay our way.

In fact, as citizens of the dream, we cultivate someone else's garden. This garden was bequeathed to us by invisible benefactors.

We may have hit upon a rich vein and we try to stay near that vein but we did not create the vein. We pray for its continued bounty. We rely upon it to sustain us. We are the honored recipients of voices whose provenance is unknown. Visions appear before us and it is our calling to form these visions and wrestle with them and cultivate them and cradle them and display them. In fulfilling that calling, we cannot expect everyone to understand what we are up to. Only other citizens of the dream seem to fully understand our economy, our sources, our methods.

Our rewards are real, but not always translatable into dollars. If we expect more than what we are getting, then we live with uncertainty and doubt no matter how grand our successes. So we treat every hearing as money. If we are painters, we treat every viewing as money. If we are comedians, we treat every laugh as money. In this way, we grow rich. In this way, as citizens of the dream, we are cared for.

This is the law that operates in the dream. Everything that we love is a kind of money. We keep track of how many people our work is capturing, and consider their attention a kind of money. That is how the economy works for citizens of the dream.

It takes faith and courage to rely on such accounting when rent is paid in dollars. And it may seem kind of soft-headed. We do not neglect the dollars. We need dollars. But as citizens of the dream we are rewarded for our work in ways that others are not.

On the minus side, of course, our lives are sometimes materially difficult. On the plus side, this currency of ours cannot be taxed. We earn it free and clear. Likewise, as creative people we have a homeland. We didn't have to take this homeland from anyone else because its land mass is infinite. It is as roomy as a dream.

But we also live on earth. Living on earth while being loyal to the dream requires struggle.

That struggle is mainly what this book is about—finding ways to live in our world of the dream while surviving in the larger world, living as aliens with quiet dignity in this supposedly real world that others inhabit with ease, and identifying others of our ilk in order to join forces with them.

The artist as solitary figure is a powerful image but we do not live alone and we do not live only in the dream; we also live in laundry and taxes. We live in real estate and disease and car payments. We live in daycare and automobile insurance and dish soap. So we need community with people who are not artists. We invite them into our world whenever we can. We do shows. We put our work out. We try to be good citizens of the dream and good citizens of the world of laundry and taxes.

I am not really a self-help guy. I do not believe we can achieve extraordinary gains from minimal effort. But I do believe in solving problems. I do use crazy things like meditation and visualization. I do assume that in the interstices of apparent contradictions lie paradoxes that can be solved.

I haven't solved them all. I'm not a philosopher. This book is full of rough edges.

HOW WILL THIS book help you in your work?

It will give you encouragement.

Sometimes all you need is to keep going. Encouragement is good for that. You may be stuck on a piece and there is no other way but to keep going.

But what good is encouragement if you're going the wrong way? Eventually you will have to change your approach.

Sometimes when we are stuck it is because we are not really present with the work. We ask ourselves, Do I feel sleepy? Am I boring myself? How can I be courageous in this moment? How can I wake up? What is true right now?

In writing this introduction, I was working over and over the first paragraph. I had to stop and ask, What is going on? I realized I was working over and over a thing that was basically boring to begin with. I had to stop and just let go of the boring thing. I had to start over. We may persist in making a boring thing more and more perfect, until we have something that is perfectly boring. Then we have to start over.

For me, writing is about fulfilling wishes. So in starting over I asked, What are my fundamental desires in this matter? It turned out that my fundamental desire is to talk directly to you about what I feel. So I went back and did that and that is what you are reading now.

I hope this is "good writing." But mostly I care that I do not feel like a liar. So that is one way of changing course. We stop and ask ourselves if we are saying what we truly want to say right now. We ask ourselves if we are boring. We ask ourselves if we feel alive.

This is true in painting and performance and music. Am I playing with feeling? Does this color or this stroke have any meaning for me? Am I likely to cry while playing this song? Am I paying attention? Am I inside the song? Do I care? What is my heart doing?

(Wow, the sun just came out. It has been raining for days and the sun just came out and it is bright on my hands through the blinds. This morning there was snow on Mt. Tamalpais and in the back yard when the sun struck the wood of the deck and the stairs and the fence out back, vapor rose from it and it looked like it was smoldering, burning from inside, and I thought about how primitive people must have considered things to be on fire after rain. How else would you interpret smoke coming off of wood? They must have considered it a special kind of burning.)

Whoops. I was paying attention to you and then I noticed the sun on my hands. I wanted you to see the sun on my hands, how it has come out after so many days of storm.

Doing so interrupted the flow. I'm not saying do this all the time. But ask yourself from time to time, What is alive right now, what matters, what is authentic?

Like you, I have had my share of problems. At times I have worked rather too close to the furnace of madness. But I have kept my eyes open.

*Cary Tennis*
*March, April and May 2011*
*San Francisco, California*

# Citizens of the Dream:

# A General Theory of Creativity

# High highs, low lows

*I'm a flaky, creative type. Should I be with
someone like me or someone more stable?*

**Dear Cary,**

I AM IN my 20s, gainfully employed, and until a month ago
in a six-year relationship with a woman. I met another woman
recently I immediately fell for but have now become good friends
with. In this process of falling in and out of a crush I realized what
attracted me to this person was the same thing that attracted me
to my ex-girlfriend and what was lacking in my soon-to-be-over
relationship.

I am a flaky creative type and when I am around people like
me I feel like I'm capable of just about anything and this was
how I began to feel after making this new friend. It dawned
on me that I hadn't felt this way the whole time I was in my
last relationship and thus should've ended it a long time ago.
Fortunately my ex-girlfriend took the news better than I thought
she would and we still share an apartment and are both enjoying
our freedom. She has even offered to take me back when I come
to my senses.

I feel like the me I knew years ago, but lately I have started to
see the darker side of being a flaky creative type again. While the
highs are really quite high, the lows are very low. When I'm not
doing painting, writing, playing music, etc., I am drinking more
than I should and in a generally foul mood. My last relationship
was very safe and middle ground and at times a bit boring, but
I always felt I could be alone and not break down. I feel that I

am at a crossroads—do I find another flake like me, do I go back to a "safe" relationship, or do I just become a crazy old hermit? Should flakes be with flakes?

*Flaky P. Creative*

## Dear Flaky,

IT DOES SOUND like you're at a crossroads. But if you're a creative type, you should probably start pricing houses there. If you're a creative type, the crossroads is where you live.

Regular folks just drive on through the crossroads. They're going somewhere smart and important. Creative types stop in the middle of the intersection and say, gee, check it out, there's a lot of energy here! The crossroads is where Robert Johnson met the devil, after all. So get yourself a lawn chair and put it on the traffic island. You're going to be there a while.

The ability to live at the crossroads is the key to creative endeavor. I know you were only speaking metaphorically, and that you really want to solve your romantic entanglements. Still, what I'm saying is that you don't necessarily have to solve your entanglements; you just have to learn to be who you are, do what you do, and live through it with calm and focused integrity. You get what I'm saying? The reason you want to do that is because what's really important is for you to be doing your painting and your music.

It troubles me, however, that you call yourself a flaky creative type, because it sounds like you're selling yourself short. It's possible you're just flaky, but if you were just flaky, I don't think you'd call yourself a flaky creative type. I think you'd probably just shut up and drink. I think you may be genuinely creative but ashamed of your inability to manage your affairs the way normal people do. If so, you don't need to apologize. But you do need to accept your talents and your limitations. You need to design your life accordingly. And you need to get to work.

4

On that note: Do you need to surround yourself with wildly creative people whose excited chatter fills you with a sense of endless possibility? No, you don't. Is it a good idea for your mate to be just as wild-eyed as you are? No, it's not. Don't fritter away your creativity in witty conversation. You need to find that sense of endless possibility in your work itself. I know what you're talking about, that with similarly imaginative people you feel you can soar. But all that soaring doesn't get you anywhere. You land with empty pockets, just like you started with. If you're a creative person, the only thing that gets you anywhere is the work. And to do the work you need a stable but stimulating environment. That's why you live at the crossroads.

You don't say much about your own feelings in all this. Again, if you're a creative type, perhaps your focus is on finding some order in the sounds and shapes that appear spontaneously in your mind. So you might be a little retarded in the area of human relationships, particularly relationships with women. If your girlfriend loves you and understands you and is willing to take you back, it might be the best thing for you. Creative, sensitive but emotionally unsophisticated men get hurt easily in relationships; it's sometimes better to settle down with someone you love, even if she doesn't always make your head spin. Otherwise, you spend so much precious time just trying to get comfortable emotionally that the rest of your life suffers, and you never get around to doing the work. And the work is what's important. You have to dedicate yourself to the work. That will keep you sane.

> Choose an artistic path and stay on it.

You label yourself flaky and creative, and society lets you off the hook a little. You're not expected to dress in a suit and tie and show up 9 to 5. But in return, you have to produce. In producing, you not only keep your half of the bargain with society, but you keep yourself from going mad.

So make a commitment. Choose an artistic path and stay on it. That's the best chance you have for happiness. Choose a

relationship that works for you—don't expect it to give you ulti-
mate happiness—that's what your work is for. And if the devil
greets you at the crossroads and offers to tune your guitar, tell
him no thanks, you can tune it yourself.

# Can a former ugly duckling become a handsome leading man?

*I found my calling and fell madly in love with my scene partner—but then I got scared and went back into my shell.*

**Dear Cary,**

ADOLESCENCE WAS TOUGH on me, as it was on many. I had braces and my gums puffed up like a puffer fish; I was very overweight ... I felt like the ugly duckling. The high school I attended was full of wealthy, beautiful kids who for the most part were not cursed by awkwardness such as mine; I turned to computers as a means dis-identification from my sister and shunned all things "creative." Although I always had an eclectic group of friends, I felt like an outcast. As high school ended I lost a big chunk of weight. I went to college and my weight fluctuated over the next four years along with my eating, drinking and exercising habits. One thing remained constant though: I had no success with the ladies.

Years ago, a seed was planted in me, a seed that I never allowed to develop because I never felt worthy. My whole life, I wanted to be an actor. But who wants to watch a fat, awkward teenager? No one, I thought, so I avoided it and buried myself in science and math. So after 18 months in the real world, I said, Fuck it! and took a very intensive acting class. The classes have been cathartic to say the least. But I have reached an impasse of sorts;

I have actualized the appearance of the man I wanted to be, but it stops there. It isn't really me yet.

My latest class, I was blessed and cursed with an incredibly beautiful scene partner. The scene we did was simple yet beautiful and compelling; moreover, it forced me to go to the dark places and dust out some cobwebs. The scene itself opened me up to a part of myself that I had put on lockdown and helped me immensely as an actor and in the process I fell head over heels for my scene partner. That's when disaster struck: Once our scene was complete, I turned to ice on her; it reminded me of what rejection and pain felt like, and I ran for the hills as fast as possible. Part of me thinks that she may think she upset me in some way, another part of me thinks she was never even into me in the first place, and then the saddest realization of all sets in: It's not about her. It's about my inability to make a connection with another human being. I'm so scared of what might happen that I never let anything happen.

Do I just bare my soul to her, let it all out? Do I try to repair the damage I've most likely done? I want to open myself up to her, to tell her—no, show her who I am and why I went cold—but I'm afraid that's asking too much of her. I want her to understand me, but I'm afraid that it will be too much, but I need to tell someone. I need someone to understand so I don't feel so alone.

*Duck on a Pond*


Dear Duck on a Pond,

FIRST OF ALL, I want to say that however panicked and afraid and confused you feel, these feelings won't kill you. You have chosen a kind of work that will bring much emotional turmoil; that is part of the work. So you need to maintain a kind of clean room within yourself, a place where you know that no matter how crazy and tumultuous you feel, you are still going to be OK. After you are done with a scene, go to that room that you keep for yourself. Ground yourself. Take some breaths.

Like I say, these feelings won't kill you. Obviously, in acting, you have found the key to becoming the complete person you want to be. That is your dream. Keep following it. The only thing that will kill you is not following your dream.

I can't say what to do about this woman in particular. Her feelings will govern what happens, and nothing you do right now will change her feelings. Don't worry that you did something wrong. What's important is that you acted well.

This pattern will probably become familiar to you: As you work to express a scene, you draw on deep emotional reserves. In doing so it will feel as though you are falling in love with your partner. Perhaps you really are falling in love with your partner. It doesn't matter whether we call it real or not. Perhaps the more real it appears, the better—although you must maintain control over it or it is not acting. The point is, there will always be a bit of a shock when the scene is over. There will be some territory you must traverse, high above the rocks, where you are neither in the scene nor in your ordinary life. Part of your job as an actor will be to learn to traverse that vertiginous offstage space with some grace and surefootedness. Otherwise, acting will be too difficult. You will not be able to find your way back and forth from your daily life to your scene; you will get lost somewhere in the middle, and you will miss too many auditions.

> Maintain a "clean room" within yourself.

Acting can be a route to the truth. Because you are acting, you are allowed to be authentic. Eventually, what you discover about yourself through acting will become less exotic; it will slowly become part of who you really are. You were surprised when you turned to ice once the scene was complete. But that makes perfect sense: Acting kept you warm. Ideally, you will learn to bring some of that warmth into your daily life. But this will happen gradually.

I think you are going to have an intense creative life; your main challenge will be to manage the psychic dramas that you stir up in order to succeed creatively. This is not at all unusual. The difference between creative success and failure sometimes has less to do with talent itself than it has to do with how well we traverse the void. Many cannot handle the journey back and forth; we get lost in the chill between acting and doing.

So don't freak out. That clumsy, frozen awkwardness: It comes with the territory. Keep working at your craft. Remember that you are moving back and forth between serving the needs of the drama and serving your own needs. It will be confusing at times. It will be terrifying. But those feelings won't kill you.

What will kill you is if, at this crucial moment, you turn away in fear. Acting is what you need to do. Keep doing it.

# I'm restless and creative but don't know where to begin

*I see this dazzling world full of art and fun—how do I connect to it?*

**Dear Cary,**

I'M 24. I graduated from college two years ago, moved to another state to pursue my career in graphic design, worked for a year and a half and was in a serious relationship for a while, broke up with the boyfriend, moved back to the state I went to college in, and now here I am. I have no regrets, even though I have been mostly unemployed for the three and a half months I've been back. It's still one of the best and most fulfilling decisions I've ever made. So I'm more at peace with where I am than ever before and happier than ever to be single, but now my other haunting thoughts are bugging me more than ever.

I'm always, always, always yearning for more in my life. My life and I have always been just plain mediocre. I don't want a "simple life," and my longing for more has grown steadily over the years. When I try to think about what exactly it is that I want, I can't figure it out. To name some things that are somewhat tangible—I browse the social Web sites and see people who have/do things I'd like, such as involvement in the local music community and events, fun and creative friends, trips to fun places, interesting lifestyles, successful and happy relationships, talent in music, art or languages, etc. And I have these strange feelings all the time, like I want to sit down and write a song or a poem or create something, but I don't know where or how or what ... or why.

Maybe if I meet new people, I can be introduced to new, exciting things. But meeting people or making new friends scares me. It makes me exhausted just thinking about having to get close enough to new people to be myself around them ... and then they might sense my mediocrity and not like me anyway. Strangely, I'm a shy introvert who craves social community, similar to what I see in churches (minus all the stereotypical problems that come with that). But the process of meeting a group of people makes me want to hide.

I feel guilty, because I know I am lucky/blessed to have the life I have. I have good health, good friends and family (although most of my friends are married now and I don't see them much), a roof over my head, and all of the basic important things that some people don't have. But every time I put aside this feeling of longing as disguised greed or silliness, it doesn't go away. It comes back. Often.

I've started to write this e-mail about 20 times over the past two years, and I've always stopped. I don't know if it even makes sense, but this time I decided to finish it and send it. Hopefully you can give me some perspective. Am I just being a self-centered whiner? Maybe these are common feelings? Is there something obvious I'm missing about myself that is evident in what I'm saying? What can I do to feed this hunger? I'd really appreciate hearing your opinion. I really need to start moving forward.

*Thanks, Wanting More*

Dear Wanting More,

TO ANSWER YOUR questions, I don't think you are a self-centered whiner, and these are fairly common concerns. But the artistic temperament is often restless. Your friends and family may indeed not understand some of your restlessness. They may think that you should just chill out. Well, I'm sorry, but creative people do not easily chill out. All you can do is accept that you have to be working on creative projects and you have to be among other creative people, and there's nothing wrong with that, and set about to do it.

This may be the "something obvious" you are missing about yourself that is evident in what you are saying. You say it here: You want "involvement in the local music community and events, fun and creative friends, trips to fun places, interesting lifestyles, successful and happy relationships, talent in music, art, or languages, etc." You also say it here: "I have these strange feelings all the time, like I want to sit down and write a song or a poem or create something, but I don't know where or how or what ... or why."

So there you go. That's the situation. You know what the situation is. But you have not started taking the necessary actions yet.

So what you need is a method of getting from here to there. What you need is a way of taking action.

Taking action requires you to be kind of stupid. Well, not stupid, but obvious. It's so simple it sort of surprises you. You just go and be where the creative things are happening and you talk to people.

> Permission is hereby granted to go forth and bother people and be creative.

It's not that hard. But you have to be systematic and do a certain amount of not-so-fun drudge work, or footwork, or baby steps.

Say you want to be involved in the local music community. OK, so maybe you don't live in Austin. Too bad. I don't either. But most places have musicians. Music is made by people. So you have to go where the people are making the music and then you have to see how you can be involved. Many music organizations need volunteers. Bands need all kinds of help. You can help, in a humble way, if that is possible for you. Or, if helping a band put up posters and move their equipment, or taking tickets at the door of a festival, or doing any of the other million things that volunteers do in order to be connected to the scene, if none of that works for you, then you'll just have to take the step to start doing your own art. Become a net producer of artistic things.

You can form a band. That is one way. Forming a band is not that hard. You just put notices up and talk to people and start playing. At least, that's how I did it.

It helps to be driven, to want to do this really, really badly. It sounds like you do. It sounds like you want this badly enough to just do it. So do it. Do you need permission? I will grant you permission to do everything you need to do creatively. Permission is hereby granted to go forth and bother people and be creative. Whatever you have to do. That's why I moved to San Francisco, actually. I thought if I lived here it would sort of be understood if I was desperate to do creative things and embarrassed myself. It worked out for the most part, although I'm not sure you can still roll into San Francisco on a hippie bus like I did in the 1970s and get a flat at Fulton and Baker and just sort of wing it. You kind of have to have a job these days, sorry to say. But you don't have to live in San Francisco. Heck, if I was going to do it now, I'd find someplace really cheap to live. But I needed to be around people who would not kick my ass for being weird, and I wasn't sure how many places there were like that. In Florida, at that time, you sort of routinely got your ass kicked for being weird, which was why I left. But anyway, you're in a place you like, so just go start doing things. The activity will alleviate your anxiety. Just stay busy. Hang paintings. Help position sculptures. Pour wine at art openings. Learn to set up amplifiers. Hang out with people like yourself. Your activities will take an organic shape.

It would be nice, actually, if there were more formal organizations, like support groups, where creative types could just plunk themselves down and say, Hi, I'm a creative type and, uh, I'm not sure what's going on but I have to do something. I think there is something to be said for the A.R.T.S. Anonymous program, especially the idea of having an arts buddy, and making commitments to your art, and doing some kind of art in every 24-hour cycle. Of course, I'm comfortable with the whole 12-step thing, and am OK with taking what I can use and leaving the rest, but it may not be for everyone.

My main message to you, to repeat, is just to spring into action. Do not worry too much about doing it perfectly. Just begin doing things! Take concrete action in the visible world!

# I'm dying to be a musician

*Must one be born with musical talent? I yearn
to express myself but have no training.*

**Dear Cary,**

I WANT TO be a musician but I am afraid that I don't have it in me. I want to play an instrument and sing and create music and perform it. I don't really care about fame. I want to admire myself for being a more realized person, and I want to enjoy the company of artists, and until I am one I would be nothing but a fake, or worse yet, labeled a groupie. I am plagued with the existential anxiety that my life has been pointless thus far, and I see music as a way to create meaning and connection with my own humanity.

But when I listen to interviews with musicians, or hear their music, I am struck with the sense that they were born for it, that creating music runs in their veins, and that it's a way of life for them as much as eating or sleeping. Can someone become an artist after many, many years of not being musical, indeed after a life spent idling in conformity? Is a love for it and a dedication to working toward being musical every day really enough? Could someone like me really join the ranks of artists?

*I Dream of My Ideal Self, in Vancouver*

Dear Dreamer of the Ideal Self,

ABSOLUTELY YOU CAN join the ranks of artists.

Let me quote for you something from a book I am reading with great interest, called *Writing Alone and With Others,* by Pat Schneider. These are the five principles on which Schneider has based the writing workshops and the associated movement known as Amherst Writers and Artists.

1. Everyone has a strong, unique voice.

2. Everyone is born with creative genius.

3. Writing as an art form belongs to all people, regardless of economic class or educational level.

4. The teaching of craft can be done without damage to a writer's original voice or artistic self-esteem.

5. A writer is someone who writes.

Apply these same principles to music. Music is an art form that belongs to all people, regardless of economic class or education. A musician is someone who makes music. If you write you are a writer. If you make music you are a musician. And if you make music, you are not required to know the quality or the meaning of what you do, because you are giving voice to something full of surprise and mystery. You are not required nor even able to judge what you do because you are not in control of what you do. You proceed knowing only that you are giving voice to something that deserves to have a voice. And why does it deserve to have a voice? Because it is there in your body yearning to be born, trying desperately to become.

You become the body of the violin played by unseen hands.

OK, so that is a bit dramatic. But is it any more dramatic or unbelievable than the naked facts—that we humans will bang on things, blow into things, strike things and build things to make music of such complexity, order, symmetry and power that we cannot even adequately describe or analyze what we ourselves have done? Is what I am saying any more startling than the naked facts?

All I can conclude is that we are not in complete control of what we create.

It is by thinking about it in such a way that you find the courage to do it—indeed, that you find the necessity of doing it. You become as it were the handmaiden of your own desires.

For what is music? Music is banging on a can. Music is screeching pain. Music is silence, as has been demonstrated by eminent musicians celebrated by the wealthy and the fabulous. Music is a frame placed around sound. Music is the decision to listen. Music is a gathering.

And am I talking highbrow? Decidedly not. I am talking punk.

Punk was a revolutionary phenomenon in which many people who did not know each other personally came to the same conclusion at the same time: If we say we are musicians we are musicians. If we go onstage and perform we are performers.

That was the genius of the punk explosion: You do not need permission. Because no one owns music. A person may own a club, or a record company, or a stage or venue or concert promotion corporation. But no one owns music. And no one needs permission. And yet I am giving you permission. Why do I need to give you permission even though I say you need no permission? Because punk is apparently not operating in a vital and visible way in your area of Vancouver. You need the culture to say, Yes, come on, do it! If the culture is not around you, visible, exploding out of the bare brick walls of clubs, then people who ought to be punks look around and say, Where is my gathering? Where are my people? What do I do with this deafening sound in my head?

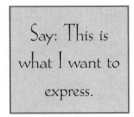

Say: This is what I want to express.

You go and play.

To play an instrument you need an instrument and you need hands. You put your hands on the instrument and make sounds come out. You listen to the sounds and make more of the sounds you like and less of the sounds you don't like. You let it speak. It may speak in an angry voice, or a frightened voice; it may speak first in a disorganized way; it may be hard to understand what it is saying. But you let it speak. You put your hands on the instrument and you let the sounds guide you to the voice. The voice will increase. It will say things that surprise you. It will thank you for allowing it to speak. It may also say things that you don't like. It may say things others don't like.

Soon you will find there are things the voice wants to say that you don't know how to make the instrument do. So you will seek instruction. But seek it on your terms. Say, This is what I want to express; how do I make this instrument make these sounds? You might say, This is what I want to say! and in demonstrating what you want to say you must leap around like a frog, flapping your arms like a chicken, or lying dead in a ditch, or flying. You say: This is what must come out of the instrument! How do I find this in the instrument? Where is it hidden? You might pay for this instruction or you might find it by forming principled relationships with other people who make sounds come out of instruments. If you like the sounds they make, then find out how they are made.

Some sounds are pure machine, stark and godlike. For instance, a Fender Stratocaster is a musical machine that makes a certain sound. A Marshall stack is also a musical machine. If a Stratocaster is leaned up against a Marshall stack and both the Stratocaster and the Marshall stack are set to maximum volume, a certain sound will emerge. This is the sound of the machines. It is terrifying and overwhelming and glorious, like a thunderstorm. You stand back a certain distance and watch it rain. Then you step in and begin to manipulate the sound these machines are making; you become a respectful intermediary between the machines. The sound belongs to the machines. You serve to shape their anarchic, joyful interaction.

On the other hand, you can bang on a can.

Punk allowed people who had the spirit and the intense desire to express themselves to express themselves in a way that did not require formal practice and training. Punk created a language and a method, and thus encouraged those who otherwise would have been discouraged. I was lucky enough to observe punk in the mid—to late 1970s and early 1980s, and to participate as a musician and later as a journalist in the eclectic avant-garde or new wave that surrounded it and in a sense followed it, took courage in its advances.

We repurposed what we could scavenge from the culture in order to create for ourselves a world of glamor and danger that reflected back to us our visions, sometimes dark and surreal, sometimes silly, always essentially private in origin and thus mysterious and full of danger. It was an amazing time, to see a small, disenfranchised group of people expose their private nightmares on the public stage and find recognition: Yes, we all feel mostly mad, yes, we are all going insane with frustration and anger, yes, we all feel impotent to change the government. It had much in common with other spontaneous and intoxicating artistic movements. One is very lucky to have been there for it. It is one of those things one takes to the grave, clutching to the chest with gratitude.

So you need a rehearsal space and you need a culture. If you begin to do it, people will recognize what you are doing and they will come around, curious, tentative, like cats. Like cats, they may act dismissive. But they will be watching, and listening through the walls.

# I don't feel like writing. Does that mean I'm not a writer?

*Every time I start to work on my second novel,
an enormous laziness descends upon me.*

Dear Cary,

I AM A young, talented writer. (You should know how much effort it took me to write that sentence without any auto-excuses built in.)

It took me a lot of time and courage to figure out that I was writer in the first place, since I have been struggling with a low self-esteem for a long time. But here I am, 31, knowing what I want to do, where I want to go.

I got my first book published in 2002, a youth novel, and it was received well. I got married and became a father, and I have a full-time day job now to support my wonderful family. And he lived happily ever after? No.

Since my first book got out, surprise surprise, I haven't been writing anymore. Plenty of ideas, but I just didn't manage to commit myself to it. When I met the young author David Mitchell last year, it was so inspiring that I started again. But three chapters into my second novel, I bailed out, stopped.

It is not that I'm stuck in the story I want to write; it still has plenty of energy. But whenever I even think of writing, I feel this huge laziness coming up, like some old man with a heavily sighing voice says, "I just don't feel like it." It looks like I need outside stimuli to write; the power to start working again does not come from the inside. Strange.

Am I lazy? Am I afraid of failing? Do I lack the discipline, the artistic urge, the necessity? Am I not a writer after all? Should I give up writing and learn to be happy without it? These questions drive me crazy sometimes.

I feel like the man in Kafka's *The Trial* now, the one who waits all his life before the doors of the courtroom of his trial but never really gets in. I feel stuck, standing still like this. I know that I could be happy if I gave up writing, but I know that I would be missing something, too. Does that make sense?

If we have a talent, are we obliged to develop it? Or are we free to not use it at all?

G

Dear G,

YOU KNOW, TO me it seems possible that all the dire things you imagine could be true, and you could still write. You might very well be lazy, afraid of failure and undisciplined and still write. You might lack the urge and still write. You might not be "a writer" and still write. After all, a writer is just someone who writes.

It is also true—now that we are at the task of arranging apparent contradictions in ingenious ways—that you are both obliged to develop your talent and free not to develop it. That is, you are free to acknowledge but defy obligations; you are free to say no to obligations.

I personally do believe that, as a guide to right living, we do have an obligation to develop our talents. But this is largely a practical rather than a moral matter for me. I do not think so highly of myself as to assume that the world will be greatly improved by my contributions. But I have observed that mastery of a craft is personally satisfying, and that failure and frustration are not. So I stick to writing and music, and do not paint or draw.

You are free. That is the thing. You are free not to write if you so choose. But you are not alone. Your choices matter to others. And the choices of others matter to you. I say this by way of getting at this notion that your inspiration should come only from some tiny, esoteric writing gland behind your navel. As a writer, you are dependent on others. You could not have published your first book alone. Why should you believe that you can write without

You are free. But you are not alone.

any external stimulus? If you need to meet with a writers group, enroll in a class, arrange with a mentor or writing friend to share work on agreed-upon deadlines, or if you need to work out a schedule of deadlines with your editor or agent, then please do so. This is often the case. The idea that a writer

works only from inner inspiration is, I think, a bit of a romantic myth, rooted in the idea of writer as solitary and mysterious hero. The writer may be that, but he is also a person in a web of community, and he is also fallible. He may be lazy and unable to meet deadlines; he may be, as I am, fearful of completion. So there is nothing wrong with building into your life some structures that compensate for your weaknesses. We are not supermen. We all need a little help.

As to this interesting voice you hear, this heavy sighing, I will say, as I believe I've said before, that only after I did a short course of cognitive therapy did I realize that the voice I was hearing, the one that said "I can't write!" and "My writing sucks!" had an actual historical source, and that the veracity of that statement could be objectively weighed against the evidence.

It may be true that you don't feel like writing. You are probably working hard and have many duties as a father. So there will be times that you have to write even though you don't feel like it. In that sense, writing is like your other roles in life as a worker and a father and a husband: It requires you to do things you don't want to do.

You do it because that is your role. It's the only way you can get anything done.

I hope this is of some help. Good luck with the next book.

# I'm afraid I'm doing
# the wrong art

*Should I paint, or sculpt, or write? I can't decide.*

Dear Cary,

I'M WRITING WITH a question that may seem silly given the current state of affairs of the world, but it's something I think about quite often, and has bearing on my own life. I think I may be in the wrong art. Even writing that, I see there is so much doubt I have about myself. When I was young, I always gravitated toward art (the craft/art kind) as my fun, free, imaginative activity of choice. I never was that good at it, never the art star in class. I was about average, but I did summer programs in art (though when I think about it, I often chose activities that weren't art, to "expand myself," when I would have probably just enjoyed tooling around in the art I already knew), and even studied in some of the most beautiful places in Europe, where I learned that I was better than I thought, if I put time into it. I was praised for my academic skills and writing, though, and even won some awards in those.

I always felt writing was second nature to me, whereas art was something that I judged myself on by myself because others didn't give me the "automatic" positive feedback they did about writing. When I was 12 or 13, I decided to make a massive sculpture in the basement, and worked on it alone for a week or three of a summer. When I think back to that time, I think of myself as someone who was discovering what she was born to do, motivated enough at a young age to work alone in a basement and be blissful. I never finished the project, but I named it, and it remains in the basement of our house. I'm not sure why I never finished it. But it's confusing because I have always felt more at home in writing communities. You know when you feel as if some group is your tribe? I feel as if writers are my tribe, but not the artists. I'm not a crazy, free, liberated person who is in the artist tribe. I've taken classes at a bunch of schools, and visual language is not the easiest for me to express myself in. But nothing makes me feel more peaceful than visual art and crafts. Cary, the weirdest thing happened to me this year. I decided to go to a life-drawing session. I had not done that kind of work for a while. I've taken classes over the years. In some I feel totally blocked. I feel so blocked that I don't even admit to the teacher that I've had training. I can't get anything out. In other classes I did eventually produce some good stuff. Anyway, I went to this drawing session. For the first few minutes I felt pretty elated to be there. I was freely drawing with the charcoal. But after about 10 minutes, this wave of exhaustion swept over me and I was overwhelmed. I left. I was pretty shocked at that feeling. I honestly do not know why it came or what its message is to me. If I'm doing something I supposedly love, why did it drain me so? Is it because I was coming up against some kind of blockage? It's been almost 10 years since I tried painting again (and I don't even really even know if I like painting). I still feel confident about crafts. People always said I was so creative, I was always the one carrying out creative projects in a group, and I always idolized art school(ers). Yet I never felt entitled, in some way. So over these years I've pursued various literary things, professionally and educationally. It's cool, but there's something that feels uptight to me about it, something I don't even feel comfortable fully admitting that I'm doing. Maybe it's too connected historically for me with the approval rating from the parents/teachers, and maybe I idealize art so much as the area of freedom. And Cary, I do believe that expressing oneself in any medium, whatever medium it may be, is a blessing, and in theory I don't really care that much which it is. Yet, something needles me, something makes me wonder if (as I consider future graduate work) I am missing the point. Maybe I am on the wrong parallel path; maybe I have chosen the safer route. Yet I get confused when I think that I am in the tribe of writers after all. I was thinking recently how much I love color and texture, and writing doesn't really have these things in the same way. And I know that if I put more time into art, I'd get better. I just wonder, somewhere along the line, did I give up because I didn't feel good enough? Yet if writing persisted, that's for a reason, too, right? No one is forcing me to do that. Cary, am I in the wrong art? Could I have been a free diva all these years? I hate feeling as if I could have been good at something else by now. But the funny thing is that I don't even do art anymore. I never felt I had to do it or else I would die. It was just something I really enjoyed doing. Maybe I should keep it as a hobby and it would be less stressful. So I haven't done it now for a long time, and others still ask me why I stopped. I don't know what I'd do art about, and I certainly don't know why it has taken on this role in my life that is so fraught (I can navigate more freely in the creative writing world, where I've been more accepted). And I also don't know why I am not motivated enough to actually do the work itself, in any medium. I see creative people doing commercially creative work: editors, graphic designers, etc. I feel that I could be one of them, but I also feel that I don't want to make my art commercial; I don't even know if I could. How should I proceed? Thank you, Cary.

*Sitting and Wondering*

Dear Sitting and Wondering,

YOUR QUESTIONS DO not seem to be so much questions as sparks and flares thrown off by an anxious mind. That is why I ran your letter at full length. It shows your concerns and worries looping back upon themselves and suggests a maddening labyrinth of uncertainty. In their shape and manner your questions tell more than they ask. You say, I feel this, I feel that, I have this history and that, and ... so ... what do I do?

I can't tell you what to do. But I can suggest ways of enduring the many strange and frightening sensations that arise in creative work. I hope you won't think I am kidding around when I do this. I sense that you are a very talented, ambitious and bright person, who is caught in a web of anxiety and fear. But I have an unorthodox way of responding. I hope you do not think it too cheeky.

You say, "I think I may be in the wrong art."

Let's make this more concrete. Let's say you are in a museum and you look around and realize, I think I may be in the wrong room. So you go to a guard and you say, "Excuse me, I think I may be in the wrong room." And the guard asks, "What room did you want to be in?" And you say, "I'm not sure. I just think I may be in the wrong room."

Now say the guard is Wittgenstein. So he says, "I think you are in the wrong word."

I am in the wrong word? you think to yourself. I am in the wrong word?

"What word did you want to be in?" asks the guard.

"I wanted to be in the right word."

"Pick a word," says the guard.

"Fabulous," you say.

"Right this way," says the guard.

"I meant that sarcastically," you say.

"Oh," says the guard. "So you want to be in the word 'fabulous,' but sarcastically. So what will you wear?"

"I will wear a sarcastic gown."

"Very good," says the guard. "You are now free to go."

Does that make sense? Perhaps not. OK, let's approach it like this:

Maybe this condition of worry and uncertainty is not connected to doing art or not doing art. Maybe this condition of worry and uncertainty is just a condition of worry and uncertainty. If we approach your condition of worry and uncertainty as a phenomenon in its own right, perhaps we can come up with some remedies.

Maybe, you say, I am an artist prone to worry and uncertainty, and sometimes paralysis, and difficulty making firm decisions and deciding on a course of action. So maybe I will work directly on the behavioral problem, by seeking ways to lessen the symptoms of anxiety. Maybe I could meditate to regulate my breathing and heart rate. Maybe I could learn to manage my time so that I do not feel so rushed. And maybe that would help me get back to work.

So try this. Try turning your questions into statements of fact. Try saying, OK, this is what I feel. I feel grief, and now I will get back to work. I feel left out. I feel doubt. I feel uncertainty. So I work. I work to give shape to my uncertainty. I work to find some voice for my doubt. I act it out. I chisel it into something. I find a form for it. I feel these things and then I get back to work.

You are flooded with awareness of things that are unknowable. As if to stop the flood, you ask a question. But unknowable things are the ground we walk on. They are the air we breathe. They make up the conditions of life.

> The answer is to pick something and get to work.

It is as if you say, I am alive and I breathe air. Now, therefore, should I draw or should I write?

The answer, as always, for an artist, is to pick something and get to work. If you have a piece of marble ready to work on in the basement, and you have your tools, then go to the basement and start working on the sculpture. If you are sitting at a desk and you have paper in front of you, start writing. If you have tubes of acrylic paint in your taboret, and there is good light, and you have a canvas stretched on your easel, then paint.

What happened to you in the painting class interests me. As we work we are often flooded with uncomfortable feelings. As we work we learn to know these feelings and use them. Creative work is exhausting. You must train for it. You must stay in shape. Life drawing is hard. At first you will feel exhausted. You are using a part of your brain that has not been exercised lately.

So be careful not to misinterpret your exhaustion as an indicator of your talent or lack of it, or of an innate disposition toward this or that medium, or as a mystical sign. It is more physical. It is more about the work. Your exhaustion and fears and technical limitations are just hurdles to overcome. The vision and the determination are what count. So focus on what you want to create. Do not focus on your technical ability or lack of it. Focus on your vision and work toward it. As you work toward your vision, let it show you what technical skills you need.

The problems to which you must apply your talents lie in the material and its resistance to you. It has its own answers. Your job is to work on the material in front of you. The answers are inside it. It will not disclose its answers to you unless you do the work.

There is always the risk of failure and always the risk of being wrong, and as you work nightmarish phenomena may occur in your mind. What do you do with those things? Do you paint them? Do you stop to write them down? Do you call a friend and talk about those things? That is up to you. The point is that you just work.

How do you know if you are doing the right work? Please, my friend. Let's have a laugh about that. That is the big joke that is played on all of us. The artist decides what is the right work. It involves some faith: I may not know what the fuck I'm doing, but I'm doing it.

I like to pretend. Let's pretend I'm the sculpture teacher. I walk around looking at what people are doing. "Why are you sitting on that block of granite, not working?" I ask. "Are you tired?" "No," you say, "I just don't know what to do." "What to do?" I say. "The answer is inside the stone. You chisel away, looking for the answer in the stone."

# Writing is in my blood, but how do I know if I'm any good?

*What if I have no talent? How can I find out?
Who can tell me?*

**Dear Cary,**

AS OF LATE, you have answered many questions from aspiring or professional writers, and every time I have hoped it would include an answer to the pressing question in my life, but it has not. The writers who have been writing you, lately, are already certain that they have talent. They suffer from writer's block, they're aggravated that their talent is going unnoticed, they wonder how to integrate writing into their lives. I am in a much earlier stage, at least psychologically. I have committed my life to writing, and I have no idea if I'm any good. What it comes down to is this: How can you tell if you have talent? I submit to magazines and they reject me. I submit to contests and I lose. I try for the creative writing awards at my university every year, and never get so much as an honorable mention. I work and work and work on my craft. I read and read and hope to absorb skill by osmosis. Everyone says this is normal, and no indication that I'm in the wrong life trajectory; this is how all writers begin. But that's obviously not true—my peers seem to be shooting by. I know I will always write. It's in my blood. But when should I give up on making a career of it? When should I stop trying to send it into the world, and keep it shamefully to myself? How can I tell if I'm just part of the pathetic, misguided slush that clogs the mailboxes of magazines? There is a line from *Little Women* that always stuck with me, after reading it as a child. Laurie is trying to write music like Mozart, and he realizes: "Talent is not genius, and no amount of work will make it so." He goes into business.

There must be someone who could read one of my manuscripts and then whack me across the face with it—or tell me, yes, keep on trying, there's something here. Where do I find him?

*A Writer or a Fool*

Dear Writer or Fool,

ONE DOES NOT write only to display one's talent. One also writes as a spiritual practice and a mode of self-discovery. One writes in order to see. One writes in order to remember. Writing is like a sixth sense used to apprehend a reality not detected by the other five. It is the memory-sense, or the feeling-sense, the organ through which we make known to each other a rich world not otherwise knowable. It is also the medium through which we make known history and the soul of our culture. It keeps something alive that otherwise might die. It is an important act regardless of whether it gains an individual writer fame and praise.

So if you are writing, and if writing is, as you say, in your blood, your question about talent is moot. It is more a question about how you persist in writing through the fear, discouragement and disappointment that are endemic to the activity.

Logically, it works out like this. All the practice you get makes you better. Whatever stops you from practicing makes you worse. One thing that may stop you from practicing is the belief that you are no good. So the belief that you are no good may prevent you from becoming good—unless you persist in writing. Many of us wake up believing we are no good and persist anyway, knowing that if we do not persist through our feelings of worthlessness then surely we will get nowhere. Our beliefs about our value are meaningless. Writing is a thing that must be done. In doing it, we often get better. It is not guaranteed how much better we will get by daily writing. How good we get, who knows? How long it takes, who knows? But surely we will not get better by not writing. So to keep at it is a logical necessity.

It is also a personal necessity if it is, as you say, in your blood.

These are not trivial matters.

The related question is one of professional competence and success. There is no guarantee of success for talented writers. Success is a whole other ball game.

But let's back up. It is important to talk about how we persist in doing the most demanding writing. I have for seven months been holding writing workshops at my house. So naturally I have been thinking about the creative process and why the Amherst Writers and Artists method works. One reason I think it works is this: For reasons psychological, spiritual and philosophical one must learn, through practice, to regard  one's creative work with some compassionate detachment, and not to equate it with one's own worth as a person. We are attempting to contact a source beyond our conscious control. So we must be willing to be surprised by what we find. In order to be surprised, we must have some distance. So in the workshop we try not to address the creator of the work directly. We talk about the work as if it were separate from the creator. The hope is that this will allow the creator also to gain some distance from the work, to be detached as it unfolds. Otherwise, ego fear emerges. The ego will try to remain separate and distinct; it will impede and filter; it will try to steer us away from things that resonate with other people. The ego is too concerned with its place in the world. You need something broader and more subtle to act as your guide. You need a method that encourages you to gain detachment from the work.

I think much good writing, of the kind I like now as opposed to the kind I liked when I was younger, is very simple writing. In writing this column I have come to love the unadorned voice of the letter. I have come to love the subtle variations in individual voices that indicate who is speaking. They are not reducible to tricks of style. They seem more like that complex and undefinable combination of traits that we think of as individuality. I have come to love the individual and untutored voice.

There is a political dimension to this. One of the fundamental assumptions of a society that wishes to live in liberty is that individuals matter. That means the lowliest person matters. When we accord value only to the high, the famous and obviously accomplished, we endanger the esteem in which the lowly are held. So I say give more esteem to the low. So give voice to the voiceless. Help the voiceless find their voice. This is work that helps our society as a whole. It strengthens those on the bottom.

And, damn it, most of all, if you are in doubt as to what you have to say or why you are writing, it must be true that each of us has some searing white-hot core of feeling and being that is trying to find its way to the surface. It may seem alien to us; it may frighten us if we identify it with ourselves. So we must have a method by which we can assure ourselves this white-hot core of our being is not something to fear, that it may be something individual to us or it may be part of the voice of our species, the collective voice of humanity in all its pain and grandeur. It may be our desire to survive. It may be our primordial sense of existence. It may be a prenatal consciousness. It may be childhood's first glimmer of separate being, our love of beauty, our sense of the divine, our wonder and amazement, our most secret and delicious ecstasies, our most fervent beliefs, our moments of pure being, our strange battles in the night, our dreams, our best meals.

It may take a while scratching around on the surface to find those things and coax them up. But writing, if undertaken seriously, strips away layer after layer, making it more likely year by year that something of this white-hot core of being will emerge. You scratch the ground year after year hungrily looking for something good. You exhaust what is on the surface. You keep pawing away, you keep digging, you keep staring, you become uncomfortable in your chair, you think you hear a voice from beyond, you think you see the glimmer of a ghostly nightgown in your family home bending over you in your bed, you become distracted, you watch the dog moving about the yard—there is the dog draped like a courtesan on the deck, her head hanging over the redwood edge, contemplating a bug traveling across the concrete step, her white fur mottled in the shade of the camellia and the tea tree; you notice the yellow clover and green grass and lavender, the April air impossibly fresh and clean, and suddenly you realize you have scratched away and scratched away and have found traces of a lost world and then were hurtled back into the now and you find—what?—you find the family dog under a flawless sky watching a bug move across the step. After mucking around in the murky past you explode into the present. You find that you exist! It may seem like not much, but it is a beginning. And tomorrow you can go again in search of that ghostly white nightgown.

This takes perhaps many years.

In the meantime, I don't believe you are ever wasting your own time writing. Some people might think you are wasting theirs, but that's their problem.

So we end up with many pages that will never be seen. But we did the work. And the work was important.

# Will our words ever
# be heard again?

*We write and we write and we write on the Net,
dispensing thoughts and advice. For what?*

Dear Cary,

MY PROBLEM IS that we have a one-day cycle in our writing, in
our lives. You read our problems; then people read our problems
in your column. Then people read our responses, but then the
sun comes up again, and all our writing goes down on the cycle,
to oblivion.

I go nuts trying to give good advice to your letter writers, and
also trying to provide wisdom and info in other Salon topics. But
it all washes away after a single day. Smart, thoughtful posters
get their say, but raging ding-dong posters get away with their
silliness, because it all starts over again every day.

I always have imagined that future historians and archaeolo-
gists will read Salon, and gain insight on our society. But, Lord
Almighty, we have so many words on our World Wide Web, and
so many people!

Classical civilization had fewer writers than we have now, and
even fewer whose work has survived. It is possible for a person to
read every single surviving written work from all of Greek and
Roman literature. Now, though, yikes! Overall, we generate as
many words in a day as all those surviving classical works.

So! My question: Will anybody ever read what we write here,
after today? I am sure our writing will persist in the World

Wide Web, but will anybody ever read it again? Will our best, well-meant advice ever help anybody else in the future? Will our detailed knowledge ever help anybody in the future? Or do we just get filed, permanently?

And, does it matter?

*Frequent Wise Man*

Dear Frequent Wise Man,

WE DO NOT know what will be left of our culture.

I do imagine that in oral cultures a great deal of brilliant talk was made and all of it is lost. I imagine that Homer composed poems more brilliant than any that were written down, and they are lost. I imagine that throughout time seers and sages have solved the mysteries of the universe while drunk on wine or high on hallucinogens, have seen it all and tried to convey it but had no tools with which to do so, and therefore countless moments of wisdom and genius, perhaps the very keys to the universe itself, have been glimpsed and they are lost.

If you have ever had the sensation of comprehending for an instant the totality of the universe and thinking, I've got it! I see it! I understand! and then slinking sheepishly into the house an hour later with only the fuzziest recollection of what you have witnessed, then you can imagine how many times this has happened throughout history, how many solutions to the world's ills, how many poems of crystalline brilliance, how many mathematical proofs, how many perfect melodies and glistening poems and fantastic, indescribable visions of universal harmony have come to our ancestors and our brothers and sisters throughout time meditating high on mountaintops or walking along dirt paths from village to village or sitting in forest shacks and caves, or journeying in ships across vast oceans or contemplating the enormous desert sky, and you can imagine the tragedy or humor implicit in this: that it all has been lost. I imagine that many who have taken psychedelics have seen, in an instant, the very core of existence, but have not had the mathematics or the physics or the poetry to convey it, and so those visions are lost. I imagine that in the pubs of Ireland poems are composed daily by farmers in their cups and they are lost by the morning. I imagine that in New Guinea seers know with utter certainty the secrets of the universe but do not trust us or do not know us or figure we wouldn't understand anyway, and so these secrets of the universe will die with them and be lost.

At the same time, as we prattle on endlessly in our way, I imagine that software of ever-increasing subtlety will be devised to ferret out important truths from the staggering mass of words that now pile up like a digital landfill, clogging the servers of the world. I imagine that everything we have written on the Net will eventually be retrieved, sorted and priced, valued according to its originality and wit.

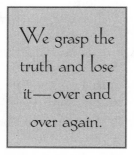

We grasp the truth and lose it—over and over again.

But does what I imagine bear any relationship to the actual future we race into as though sliding down an icy mountain? Will what we say here ever really be unearthed and used? Will there be a need for it? Are we just playing out the old fantasy of immortality, dreaming that our words will live on? And, as you say, does it matter?

I do not know, but you and I and all the rest of us go on dreaming, trying to see the order in chaos, to glimpse the perfection at the edge of madness, look for the souls of trees and hear the voices of clouds and see in each occluded heart some echo of divinity. I know that we keep on talking and writing and it goes somewhere. Perhaps in that universe that even now is spinning backward from our own, our words are coming back out of the spring air and into our mouths and back into our brains where they will lie dormant, as if never spoken, until the pre-universe universe contracts sufficiently to cause another Big Bang, and it will start all over again, and after millions of years fish will climb the rocks and grow lungs again and apes will pick up tools and invent language all over again, and again as they speak and speak they will begin to wonder, Will this ever be heard again? Will future generations benefit from all our thoughts and visions? Does any of this really matter? And again the apes will go to psychiatrists and lie on couches and fill the air with doubt and uncertainty.

So it goes. Our uncertainty and doubt extend to the infinite sky and throughout time, shrouding perfection, blurring truth, undermining what feeble faith we can muster, reminding us that we are both divine and mortal, that we live both inside time and outside time, that we are creatures of many worlds, and that we will always wonder, and always try to cheat death, and always listen for the echoes of our words in every strange town, on every strange mountain, in every strange dream that comes to us in the night.

# I peed at my desk in third grade and now I'm afraid to sing

*I know I am different. I know I go for broke.*
*What if my gift is rejected?*

## Dear Cary,

ONE DAY WHEN I was in third grade, while everyone was studying quietly, I had to go to the bathroom. I was too scared to raise my hand and break the silence and speak. Everyone would know that, right then, I had to go pee. Everyone would look at me. I thought another option was for me to quietly get up and walk across the room to the teacher's desk and ask her so that no one else could hear, but I was afraid she would get mad at me for getting out of my seat without asking first. So I just sat and held it as long as I could, but my bladder got the better of me. I peed at my desk. Obviously then, everyone really was looking at me and judging me.

A few months ago my boyfriend of two years and I broke up. I missed him terribly at first, but I've come to realize that all that time I was with him I was so scared of being myself around him that it could have never worked. Now I feel crazed with all this newfound freedom to be me again. I do things that in the past I would have been too scared or embarrassed to do, like buy pink padded bras cause they make me feel sexy, or drink wine and dance at my cousin's wedding. Everyone remarks about how much fresher and happier I seem, and I feel that it's right.

But I am a shy person, so doing new things under my general umbrella of awkwardness at life makes me feel a bit of a spaz.

I need to be able to find my center and spend time alone when I should, but I also want to be able to allow myself to guiltlessly do these crazy things I want to do.

Case in point: Recently, a friend of mine expressed interest in playing music with me. I'm a good singer, but as far as instruments go, I'm not very good yet. I told him that, but he still seemed eager to play with me. He asked me what popular songs I like to play and I was embarrassed because I don't know any. I just play whatever comes to me. I don't necessarily feel that's a disadvantage, and it's certainly not when I play by myself, but he has been in bands before and he might not think the same. I've protected the creative part of myself so long from other people out of fear of their judgment or ridicule at what I consider is the best part of me, perhaps at the cost of its own growth, thinking that letting someone hear me sing or play is like letting the person in on my secret. It may not be a big deal to him, but if I let him see this deepest side of myself and he doesn't think it's any good, I'd be crushed.

My ex-boyfriend and I used to play and sing together, and if nothing else, I really miss having that creative outlet. So I worry that I am going to try to substitute this guy for my ex. I find this person attractive and I like hanging out with him, but I've never really learned how to just be friends with guys. His eagerness somewhat befuddles me and adds to my apprehension about being friends with the male sex for fear of unknowing what he may or may not want from me. Why would he want to play with me if I can't play that well? 'Cause I'm a girl? So in that regard I am tempted to just tell him never mind about the whole thing and not chance making a fool out of myself by thinking it means something more than just playing music and being creative together. But I really want to do this.

I am still afraid about silly things, like the fact that maybe even as you're reading this you'll think I'm ridiculous and just pass it off. But I know I am organic and creative. I know when I create things I do it with all of my being. I know I have something good to share if I can just let it out. If I dance, I dance as if to bring down the house. If I sing, I sing as if to drop the moon.

I don't want to be afraid to show people who I am anymore. But I am still pretty fucking terrified at times.

*spazzy pee girl (holding it as long as I can)*

## Dear Spazzy Pee Girl,

WHEN I WAS in fourth grade, I was the kid who vomited. I was the kid who vomited frequently. I was the spazzy vomit boy. I was a worrier, an anxious boy, a boy full of private visions, terrified of the world. I do not remember much from that period; it seems that much has been erased, or lives in a kind of memory that requires intense emotion to uncover. It was 1962 and there were missiles in Cuba and we would look up at the Florida sky and wonder if death and fire were going to rain down upon us. I do know that. And I know that in my house there were money fears and fights. We were not at war. Still, the skies threatened. There were missiles in Cuba. Perhaps that was why I was so anxious.

I remember squirming in my little desk one time during that period, raising my hand, needing to run to the back of the class but afraid to do so without permission, feeling the heat well up, feeling the cold sweat on my face, feeling utterly alone and abandoned and scorned, no one to help me, no one to run to, afraid to run to the teacher because the look on her face would say that I was not to get the help and warmth that I needed, that I would face only scorn and ridicule.

So I stayed in my desk as long as I could, and then when I was starting to heave, I left my desk and started to run to the back, but of course I didn't make it, and I ended up on my hands and knees in the aisle, vomiting on the linoleum. I remember that linoleum. It was cool to the touch. I remember the stink of the vomit, so near to my face, my hot, shamed, teary face.

The question of course was, Why didn't you raise your hand?

Ha ha. Why didn't you raise your hand? But I did! I was waving my hand! You weren't looking.

Thus the child's humiliation follows him, and tied in with the humiliation of the child is the child's wounded innocence, the feeling that this was not my fault; I was trying to follow the rules, trying to be a good child, and look this is what I get: Scorn, humiliation, incomprehension by adults: Why didn't you cry out! Cry out? And what student has ever gotten a good result by crying out? When has that ever been a good idea? Why didn't you cry out? Indeed, and risk more scorn and humiliation?

Already locked into the authoritarian rows that lack all organic reason and seem strictly regimented to make us into soldiers or businessmen and not into creative souls who might want to turn their desks backward to enjoy

> Our little sufferings allow us to connect.

listening to the teacher from behind or to the side to enjoy watching the pine trees and the highway, or to sit on the floor instead of in the desk to alleviate the imprisoning influence of the desk, the desk, the desk, every day the desk, the pencils, the paper, the blackboard, the teacher, every day the hands raised, the click-clack of her hard heels, her authoritarian skirt and her authoritarian glasses, her authoritarian ruler slapped on the desk, her authoritarian calves in her authoritarian stockings, her authoritarian farts we were not allowed to comment on or giggle about lest her fury rain down upon us, her authoritarian marching up and down the rows of desks, we children putting our heads down like prisoners in solitary confinement, our tiny joy at our daily release, our enormous sorrow at returning again the next day, my black blinding depression and fear on Sunday Ed Sullivan nights, when tomorrow again there would be the vomitorium of the classroom, the torture chamber, the hellish prison of mechanical restraints, the swirling, blinding heat, the fear of ridicule, the desire for approval, the boredom, the tedium, the feeling that even at 9 my life is passing, passing away, that even at 9 I have nothing to look forward to, that even at 9 this is how it's going to be forever, imprisoned in a tiny desk chair among idiots, subject to the whims of a despot with a ruler who asks every Monday morning how many of us went to church yesterday, and as I do not raise my hand when I feel I am about to vomit, so I do not raise my hand when she asks who went to church.

I was the spazzy atheist vomit boy of small-town Florida.

But that was many years ago. So let me tell you what has happened in the last few hours. Let me show you, if I can, the kind of moral and creative universe I am living in, and ask if you can share this universe with me. So I have published a book and am distributing it myself. So I was at the post office at 9 a.m. filling out customs forms to send books to Adelaide, Australia, and to Singapore. When I left the post office to resume this morning's writing I was driving the convertible in the chilly fog (the car a gift from a friend who has emigrated to Hong Kong), and I received a cellphone call from a friend who wanted to arrange to have a book shipped to his uncle, a Holocaust survivor. So I pull over to talk because when this particular friend calls, we talk. And he says that his uncle the Holocaust survivor wanted to know, what are my spiritual beliefs, and how did I arrive at them, and how can I believe in anything after the Holocaust?

And so sitting in the car on the side of the road in the chilly ocean fog I talked about how it is possible to find belief in a power greater than oneself after such evil, and I thought of his dear uncle, who entered a concentration camp at the age of 11 or 12. I thought of this monstrous evil, this unspeakable crime, which was perpetrated against particular individuals but was also a crime against every person on earth.

So I am thinking about this and I am thinking about you and me, spazzy pee girl and spazzy vomit boy. Our troubles. And then after talking with my friend I do more mundane business in the world: I vote. I talk with someone about subleasing a storefront as a publishing office and writing haven. And then I come home and on the radio a Canadian man is speaking about his extraordinary rendition and torture in Syria at the hands of U.S.-connected torturers; he describes the 3-by-6-by-7-foot "grave" in which he was held for seven months. And I grit my teeth and utter a small scream, and my mouth grows grim and tight about the edges.

I think about you and me and our troubles, you, spazzy pee girl, me, spazzy vomit boy, and I see that as creative people, in the scale of things, our own personal difficulties and hurts do not matter—not in and of themselves: *They only matter to the degree that they help us to connect with others.* They matter because we use our shame and humiliation to imagine how it feels to be beaten with electrical wires, to be housed in a lightless grave for months on end, to be led to the ovens. Our little suffering is of no importance except where it allows us to connect. If we have something to offer, it is that we can use our small inconveniences to imagine great evil. If people make fun of us, ridicule us, shun us, shame us, that just helps us to imagine, magnified a thousand-fold, the humiliation of being led to the gulag, the humiliation of being stoned in the street, and how, even being stoned in the street, in the physical pain and the agony of approaching death, there is also the incongruous modesty and concern for appearances, how the victim of a public stoning reaches down and attempts to adjust her clothing to preserve her dignity in death.

In the face of that, what are our little sufferings and failures? Why am I publishing and distributing my book myself? Not because I thought it would be a fun idea. Because it failed to find favor with major publishing houses. Do I feel spurned and resentful? Yes. But do I have something to offer? Yes. Will I take the business decisions of major publishing houses as aesthetic judgments on the value of my creative work? No. I will form my own business. I will offer my work in any way I can. In scale and degree, my own difficulties finding a publisher are minuscule. In scale and degree, our suffering as creative people is barely perceptible, compared with the suffering of those who are tortured in gulags and burned in the streets and kept in prisons because of what they dared say, or write, or think, or sing.

At the age of 12 my family moved, and it was a traumatic move, and I was unhappy and wished we could have stayed where we were. Poor me. At the age of 12, my friend's uncle was placed in a concentration camp to face starvation and death. Can we understand the monstrous evil of the Holocaust? Can we understand the haunted dreams of a torture victim? Does my spiritual practice, born of necessity in the depths of a personal hell, have any relevance for a person whose spirituality was forged in the caldron of a world-historical evil against humanity?

I do not know. A person's spiritual beliefs are his own, forged in the smithy of his own conscience. All I know is that my difficulties are small, and my pains are unimportant in and of themselves; their only purpose is to help me connect with people whose suffering is great and whose pains are monumental.

This is the scale. This is the landscape. These are the historical and moral parameters in which a creative person confronts his or her fears and decides how to proceed. There is torture and genocide and evil. And there is personal embarrassment and humiliation.

This is not saintly. There is practical value in it. Considering the sufferings of others helps us forget our own fears as we go onstage or send out our writing. So we take them lightly. They are of no consequence. So bear these things lightly. Think of the greater world. Think of your ancestors and the generations to follow. Think of your gift.

With your gift comes a duty, in both senses of the word: both as an obligation and as a tax—a special tax levied on something of value brought in from afar.

There is no escaping this, so you might as well accept it now. If you turn away from your creative gift, it will not go away. It will just fester and you will become depressed.

So you might as well face it: It's not about you and how you feel. It's about the gift.

That doesn't mean your gift has to be huge. You don't need world-historical virtuosity to say you have a gift; you may have a modest gift. Still, it is a gift. It is not yours; it is entrusted to you. It is something beyond you, something you didn't cause to come into being, something handed to you. It is a gift, and with it comes a duty. Carry it lightly, but carry it.

# Citizens of the Dream:

# The Perils of Higher Education

# What am I doing here?

*I got into the hot creative writing MFA program
I dreamed of, but now I feel I don't belong.*

## Dear Cary,

SINCE I STARTED being serious about fiction writing, say about
four or five years ago, I realized there was only one thing that I
wanted. I wanted a shot at being a writer, and the way I defined
that (knowing there were many ways I could have defined it) was
to be accepted to a certain rather prestigious MFA program.

Some time after I finished college, I applied to that program
and a whole bunch of others and I didn't get into a damn one. So
I ran away from home and went abroad for a while and did some
other seemingly frivolous but actually kind of important things.
When I returned to the States, I realized I still wanted this thing.
So I gave it another shot. And you know what? I got in. I got into
this place that I'd always wanted to go; I got this reward I always
longed for and never dreamed of.

Then something really kind of poetic happened, the kind of thing
that if somebody wrote it into a story of theirs for workshop, the
class would totally not believe. Several months before I left my home
to go off into the middle of nowhere and pursue my dream, I fell
head over heels in love. (I know, I know, you totally saw it coming.)

So I moved, but I flew back a lot and he flew here a lot.
Meanwhile, I found out that my dream locale wasn't so dreamy.
I'm not sure that I deserve to be here. I can't see that my work
is getting any better. I feel like my classmates are all better writers than I am and it doesn't help that most of them have odious

personalities. I have continued to write, which in my mind is better than giving up, but I find myself constantly thinking I'm crap and wondering if I should give up this ghost.

Also, my significant other has made the decision to move and be with me. This is a big sacrifice on his part, but I am very happy about it and think it's going to be very good. We talk a lot about getting married and I know we will. Our relationship makes me happier than I've ever been in my life, happier than I ever thought I could be. In fact, it's one of those things that makes me rethink writing even more. I love this person way more than I could ever love writing, or be good at it. And ultimately my life-love relationship should and will trump any of my personal professional goals.

So what am I doing here? I'm going to stay and finish my degree, but I've been thinking a lot lately about never writing a word afterward. Does that make me a terrible person? Sometimes I am haunted by my adolescent obsession with being a writer and I feel like I am giving up on a part of me I might some day regret. On the other hand, I look at the sentences I string together, and by God, they suck! And yet I still send stories out to magazines, hoping they will think they're good and want to publish them.

I really want you to publish this letter, but part of me knows that if anybody here reads it, they'll know exactly who wrote it. And the last thing I want them to know is that I think they're all better than me. Especially because I got a special fellowship that they probably think I didn't deserve.

Maybe I'm just coming to terms with the agony of being a writer, an agony that may be too much for me to handle. Or maybe I never was a writer in the first place.

*Confused Student Writing Pathetic Fiction*


## Dear Confused Student,

AS YOU GET older, you learn things you didn't think you needed to know, or didn't want to learn or didn't think were important, or thought were beneath you.

Here is the big main thing I learned: My writing is not here to support me. I am here to support my writing.

How it came about was I endured some failure as a writer trying to make money as a writer, and had to work at other things for five years. During that time I wrote but not for money. I wrote on the subway, alone, in a notebook, sitting by myself in the crowd. I wrote to save myself.

It turned out that writing to save myself was the best way to write. Here is why, I think: Our writing is the voice of a person who is innocent, powerless and in need of protection; our writing is the voice of a person who needs to be heard as he or she really is. It is deep stuff is what I mean. And shocking as it is to say, the person who is writing this—the person I am today—is the kind of person toward whom I once would have leveled pitiless scorn.

> My writing is not here to support me. I am here to support my writing.

I was a typically arrogant grad student but I had some losses and loss became my teacher. I learned that writing is not about face. It is about soul. It is a tool for becoming who you are.

This is not something easily taught or easily learned, because it is not much fun to believe and act on, and it does not promise to bring sparkly fame. It is just something that has become true for me. Along the way, I have bumbled into this creative form that was not taught in graduate school but seems congenial to my spirit, an epistolary form not entirely new—I learned of its possibility by watching Garrison Keillor do it—but new enough not to be taught in grad school.

This perhaps will change.

So finish your degree and take care of your writing as you would take care of an animal or a child. Do not send it out into the world to do an adult's job. Just take care of it and, in its own way, it will take care of you

# Graduate schools can drive you crazy

*Why do arts graduate schools, in particular,*
*bring out our vulnerabilities?*

Dear Cary,

YOUR RECENT COLUMN on the confused student in creative writing graduate school touched me because I am going through something similar. I am studying for an MFA in sound design at one of the best art schools in the country. I always believed I would be a professional pianist, but the bottom fell out of that dream a few months before I graduated from college. A trusted teacher and mentor lied to me about my admission status into her program, and I never recovered from the blow. Looking back on this crushing blow two years later, I can see that what I needed most was for my adolescent image of a piano virtuoso to be brought down to reality to show me for what I was: a talented musician who hates to practice. It quite simply wasn't what I loved to do.

I'm not sure that sound design is my passion, but my school is opening up the artistic side of myself while simultaneously forcing me to break down insecurities and creative blocks that I've hidden behind for years. My main speed bump at this point is my high self-expectations. It's not that I even fear failure or mediocrity; I fear falling short of expectations. As we approached our final projects last semester, it was leaked that I was accepted in the highest position with the most money in my class of sound designers (though a pool of four really doesn't serve for the best comparison). The fear that my fellow designers would upset my No. 1 spot was paralyzing.

I've since managed to work through it; during three years of therapy while I was an undergrad, I realized that my conscience (for lack of a better word) actually functions. In my case, it is like a compass pointing in the right direction; all I have to do is get still enough to settle the needle. Meditation has helped me achieve this mental stillness, but as I get stressed, I meditate less though I need it more.

In any case, the anxiety of wanting to be "the best" still nags at me even as I realize there is no clear measure of artistic talent. I really took comfort in your honest story of loss. It gives me hope as I keep moving forward, discovering my talents. Thank you!

*Working a Sound Program*

Dear Sound Program,

WE CREATIVE TYPES are never going to be completely pure in motive or completely free of self-doubt or completely anything. We're going to be evolving, processing, creating, taking in the world, transforming it, moving on. We're in motion. This motion can be exhausting. And it wears down the machinery. So we need tools for maintenance and repair.

Meditation is a great tool for maintenance. I like what you say: You have to get still enough for the needle to settle. Meditation is so important for artists! Not only do you have to get still enough for the needle to settle in the sense of settling on an overall future direction, but you have to settle the needle every day. Every day I get up and hope for still waters. If I stir the waters up too much early in the day, that's it for the day. I can't see a thing on the bottom. I have to wait for tomorrow for the waters to clear.

And then there's this other thing you mention: betrayal by a trusted mentor. Betrayal causes huge damage.

I've been carrying on a sporadic correspondence with someone about a big creative betrayal that involves a powerful

American institution, and the more I think about it, the more I realize the great power betrayal can have over the creative spirit. Why is that? Are creatives more vulnerable to personal betrayal than the population at large? Why might that be? Is it because so much ego is invested in one's reputation as a creative type? Is it because we creatives are often immature? Do we lack self-protective behaviors, or insight into the motives of others? Are we naive? Are we codependent? Do we often misjudge others? And do we

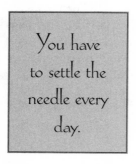

You have to settle the needle every day.

also, as creatives, carry our valuables like innocent travelers on dark roads, unaware of what others will do to get what we have?

We must look at ourselves with pitiless clarity. Like victims of con games, we must bear some of the blame. There is probably larceny in our hearts to begin with—dreams of fame and greatness, an inflated sense of our own importance. We are easily led to believe that we'll win that jury prize. We think we deserve it. We start to act as though we've already won it. Then when it is snatched away, we collapse.

Why does it take so long, for instance, for a creative person to get over betrayal? What is it about betrayal that is so hard? I think it is probably in part that it is difficult for us to find our own flaws in it, what in our own nature leads us to participate in our own betrayal. Because ... for one thing, in order to pursue our creative work, we must at times idealize ourselves, our own work, we must believe it is important because otherwise, why would we do it, and of course also the external rewards are minimal, so we compensate ... with dreams of greatness.

And oh, in your case, you mention your vulnerability to unmet expectations. You feel terrible about not meeting expectations, but the betrayal was about your own expectations. So what are expectations? They are dreams. They are not the present. We are not in the present when we are full of expectations. We build them in the future and then pose them as obstacles in the present.

This column is going to be, in a sense, incomplete, as I feel we have only touched the surface of this topic.

**TO THE READER:** This letter was part of an online series in *Salon.com* on the subject of artistic betrayal. Several columns followed which do not appear in this book. They can be found in the *Salon.com* "Since You Asked" online archives from February 2007, or by using an Internet search engine to search for "Since You Asked: Betrayal" —CT

# I got the writing fellowship—
# so now I'm terrified!

*I'm lucky, I know I'm lucky, but I don't*
*feel lucky. I just feel burdened.*

**Dear Cary,**

I AM A writer who has just completed graduate school, and I now find myself in the enviable position of having won a substantial writing fellowship. This money means that I will not have to look for a job for another year, and can instead work on finishing my first book. My relationship with my long-term boyfriend is going very well, and we plan to move in together during my fellowship year. Everything is coming up roses for me—but I am absolutely terrified. Terrified of having no schedule and no deadlines and thus no externally enforced writing discipline, terrified of being constantly needy, both physically and emotionally, when my boyfriend comes home from work (since, unlike him, I will not be exhausted from an office 9-5), terrified of the changes my life will soon face. And yet, I know this fellowship could really help me to finish my book. And I know this man is the one I want to be with.

Please, Cary, give me some advice to help me stay sane in this time of many changes. I want to be healthy and independent and happy, but I fear becoming restless and clingy, too emotional and too self-involved. I know that I am smart and can be strong enough to retain and enjoy what I love—productive writing and this wonderful man—if only I have some guidance for building my new life. I am willing to work hard. Please help me find some insight into how to create and manage balance in the midst of change.

*Seeking Balance*

## Dear Seeking Balance,

WHEN YOU SAY, "Everything is coming up roses for me—but I am absolutely terrified," you express the paradox at the heart of the creative endeavor. You have found something unexpected and true. I sort of understand this and I sort of do not.

"While strong intrinsic motivation increases creativity, surprisingly, adding extrinsic motivations—even positive ones—can actually decrease creativity," says Dr. Alice Flaherty in *The Midnight Disease: The Drive to Write, Writer's Block and the Creative Brain.*

Dr. Flaherty does not mean that only bad things should happen to good writers. *The Midnight Disease* has 263 footnotes. It's complicated.

She thinks like a doctor and a scholar. I think sort of more like a poet so I am going to try to sketch it out the way I see it. This external motivation thing:

The fellowship is freighted. It is not freedom. It is a tricky gift, a lure that could be a trap, an enticement and a reward that is also a question and a demand: Can you do it if we give you this? Will you live up? Have you got it? We think you have got it but now you'd better show us. Don't make us look like fools.

> Do not let the fellowship people look inside the singing engine.

In your heart, you have to steal the money. Think of it like this: You found the money in the street and nobody knows you have it. They all think you're going to work every day. They have no idea what you're doing. Don't think about writing. All you have to do is take care of your creative spirit. It will do the rest.

Maybe you don't call it your creative spirit. Today I am calling it the singing engine. It is that place you go that no one else can go, the place you can never remember how you got there last time, the place you go every time and every time it's new; every time you find a new way; there is no worn path and you can bring no guests.

Sometimes after going there you can't remember what happened but people are astounded by what you bring back. They give you money and say, Do it more. And you say, Do what more? And they say, Give us more like that, whatever, that thing you did that was so amazing, do it again.

And you think, How could I do it again? I don't even know exactly how I did it or what I did. But it's never the same thing. Do they know that? What do they want? They want the same thing?

Maybe they do. But you have to make the conditions.

Feel this: There is only one thing you have to do and that is protect the singing engine from the fellowship. Do not let the fellowship people look inside the singing engine. They won't look at it right. They won't know what they are seeing. They will break it. So don't let them look in there. Just thank them for the money. Give the singing engine what it needs. Protect the singing engine.

Actually I was thinking about this earlier, on the elliptical trainer at the Y where I do my thinking.

Some of it is writing and
Some is gleaming metal shavings.
Some of it is song and
Some is the sound of the singing engine spinning.
We love doing it. We wear overalls. We
Come out gleaming, bringing handfuls:
Look! Look at all this!
We love the doing and we love the handfuls.
Some of it is writing and
Some of it is gleaming metal shavings.
We shake in the machine and are excited. We
Go on a journey you can't come. We
Bring back pillows, muffins, lettuce. We

Have our hidden stories. You we
Love and we would like to make you
Happy but the engine has its own peculiar
Noise. We
Try to sort it out, we do. We
Try to make it separate. We
Try to bring you only what is
finished. But O! The sound of the
Singing engine spinning! O!

Maybe you know what I mean. There is much much much much more to it than that. My simple formulation is this: I take care of the singing engine. When the man gives me money I turn the money over. I keep the engine cool. And I limit my requests. I know what happens when I ask it for things it doesn't want to give me. It clams up. It is supercilious and superior like a Mission District bookstore clerk.

So flip the paradigm. In your mind, steal the money. Make it into found money. Forget its provenance. Ignore the strings. It is found money. Turn it over to the creative spirit, the singing engine, the muse, whatever you're calling it today. Turn it over and watch what she does with it.

# I'm an art-school dropout wannabe!

### I'm in art school but I'm freaking out about the money and about what it all means!

**Dear Cary,**

LIKE MANY OF us out here, I need some of your advice. I want to drop out of my MFA program. I have already dropped out of another grad school where I was getting a master's in library sciences. I was initially attracted to library school because I had worked for a library during college and found it quite enjoyable. Also, it seemed a pragmatic choice. I could enjoy my placid day job as a librarian and work on my artwork during the evenings. However, I got bored with library school and annoyed that some of the librarian stereotypes hold true. The fussy lack of confidence I found in the student body was disheartening. It was too easy for me. I slacked off constantly and got good grades for nothing. I started missing art. I wanted to create again. So I decided to give getting an MFA a try. I figured I would enjoy being a professor and art would be my full-time life.

I have only been in the program for about three weeks, so a part of me thinks I need to stick it out for at least a semester. However, I am panicking. I don't think I made the right decision for several reasons, the first one being primarily about money. The cost of getting an MFA is ridiculous. I cannot even think the amount of money in my head. Not to mention the loans I still owe from college and library school. I have not been sleeping well because all I can think about are these mounting loans.

I feel guilty. I feel guilty about all the money I am investing in what amounts to a self-indulgent degree. Yes, art can change people. It changed me. But I don't know if I believe in the idea of getting an education in the arts. If I really wanted to change the world I should be doing my art in the world, not hiding away in some pretentious graduate program. The more prominent artists in this world do not have MFAs. Hell, some of them don't even have BFAs. If I became a recognized artist I would be invited to teach even if I didn't have an MFA.

To top it off, it's been three weeks and I have not made a thing! I have a crit coming up next week and I have nothing. My time is taken up with classes I am not really crazy about, worrying about money and feeling guilty and depressed.

Clearly I have some good reasons to want to drop out of art school and perhaps run back to library school. I am almost done with that degree anyway, and like I said before the library is a great work environment. But I don't want to seem like a flake. I am afraid of what my parents will say, what my professors who urged me to attend art school will say. My live-in boyfriend is understandably annoyed because I can't seem to make up my mind about where I am heading. I don't want to feel like I am giving up. If I drop out I might feel relieved, but I also won't really know what to do. If I decided to drop out today I will be broke and jobless. And frankly that scares me. Your advice often isn't advice but just your thoughts. And that is what I would like to hear. Just your thoughts.

*Not Sure of Anything*


Dear Not Sure of Anything,

TREAT THIS COURSE of study as though it were a work of art that must be finished at all costs. Persevere through your uncertainty and your panic. Pay attention to the details of your subjective responses. Think about what it means to be panicking in art school. Think about what it means to be borrowing so much money, to be following the directions of teachers. That is all part of being an artist.

Think about what it means to want to be an artist. That can be your art for now. Study the lives of other artists; consider their

agonized indecision, their confusion about what role to play in life, their methods for completing their work and making a living in the world. Use this time to learn all you can. That's all you have to do.

You don't have to "produce art" now. You're in art school. This process can be your art for now. You're supposed to think and learn, acquire techniques and skills, grow and develop as a person. That's what you're doing. So go to class. Throw yourself into your problems. Believe in yourself. If art has changed you, then honor that change; make this your way of paying art back. Devote yourself to art. Be a humble servant of your craft and your genius. Do the right thing. Stick with it. Be an artist.

# I was fired for doing
## my job as a teacher

*Advice for creative types everywhere:*
*Grow a thick skin. You're going to need it.*

**Dear Cary,**

THOUGHTS ON CREATIVITY and punishment—

Thomas Kuhn bequeathed to us the concept of paradigm shift in 1962. Kuhn's ideas quickly became boilerplate, but there's an element of his thought that bears on this issue of creativity.

Paradigms are like a set of spectacles that allow information to be sensed (and thus sensible) and thus interpretable. Here's the key point: People standing in the midst of a given paradigm are unable to perceive information that paradigm doesn't explain. The majority of people obey the demands of the paradigm and don't have any problems with that.

Creative people, in whatever field or context they work, have the gift of being able to glimpse, discern and interpret information outside of the paradigm. This gift will always cause pain because that sense of "vision" allows them to see what others cannot. The gift will always cause pain because it tends to create isolation. Creative people live in worlds that are not sensible to most of those around them. The stable, dominant paradigm obeys the laws of self-preservation and will always seek to repress unknown and destabilizing information (e.g., Galileo).

The practical effect is that creative people are frequent recipients of stout beat-downs from bosses, bureaucracies and buffoons.

("When a true genius appears in the world, you may know him by this sign, that the dunces are all in confederacy against him."—Swift)

I am an award-winning teacher with a file full of student thank-you notes that attest to how profoundly my work has affected their lives. Our new program director, with the full cooperation of our grandmotherly humanities department head, fired me from my assistantship on my first day of classes. I had waited 15 years—largely because of previous traumas inflicted by school—to pursue my master's. I had to clean out my desk and stand on the side of the road with my boxes of books and wait for my wife to pick me up in the August heat. The subsequent legal wrangling revealed a Rovian capacity for deception and punishment on the part of right-thinking liberal-arts administrators whose shelves are filled with books by Foucault, Kohlberg and Belenky. Eventually, some other people with the same books on their shelves, but who understood and valued the depth of what I was doing, hired me back and it all worked out.

> We are vulnerable to betrayal whenever we mistake the nature of a relationship.

Creative people, take heart. Restrain your self-pity. You don't have a choice. How else would you live? If you could conform, you already would have. Keep your eyes glistening and your intelligence white-hot (as Rumi advises). Nurture yourself with relations with like minded people, beware the impulse for self-medication, cultivate elders who have cut trail in front of you, mentor those coming behind you, and grow what the Mohawks call "seven thicknesses of skin" because you are going to need it. This is the way it has always been.

*Betrayed and Wiser for it*

## Dear Betrayed and Wiser for it,

I WOULD ONLY mention what I realized this morning as I was thinking over various betrayals I have experienced and observed:

We are vulnerable to betrayal whenever we mistake the nature of a relationship.

For artists, every other artist is a competitor. We are vying for the same prize. This is a material condition whether it feels like it or not. So friendships between artists are fraught with complexity and the potential for deep betrayal.

When we form friendships with other artists, these friendships incubate wishes and expectations that may be deep-rooted and mysterious, invisible to us, entwined with the same mysterious existential wishes that are behind our creative activity itself.

The minute we befriend another artist, we are already in danger. We are out of control already.

Citizens of the Dream:

# Making Art and Making Money

# I'm working for a cokehead at a free arts magazine

*She promised a raise and didn't deliver,
and acts like I should be grateful!*

**Dear Cary,**

I AM WRITING to you today with an ethical dilemma. But first,
a little background: I work at a small, free arts magazine. I do
most of the writing (I have a degree in studio art and art history),
plus I do all of the secretarial duties as well. The latter has been
a source of contention between my boss and me because she has
been promising to hire a part-time receptionist to help me out
but keeps saying we don't have the money.

Well, about six months ago I applied for, and succeeded in getting, another job at a small local paper. I wouldn't be writing about
art but I'd be writing, and that's really the crux of what I want to
do. After I gave notice, my boss cried and cursed me, then came
back with an offer I felt like I couldn't refuse. Central to that offer
was a pay raise of 30 percent in six months, when I'd be sched-
uled for a raise anyway. Keep in mind, however, that I get no other
perks. Sure, she'll occasionally toss me a free bottle of wine or take
me out to dinner, but I have no paid time off or insurance, and
every vacation day I take I feel like I have to bargain for. (Even
though she's regularly out of the office, she likes for me to be there.)

But I put up with all of this because, overall, I'm happy here
and I also dread change. So when she offered to take me out to
lunch the other day, I accepted without qualms. Well, it turns

out that she invited me out to tell me that I won't be getting my promised raise when she said I would. Instead, it'll be implemented over the next three to six months as finances allow.

I am beyond angry and just hugely disappointed. My fiancé and I had planned to use the raise to help save for our wedding, among a host of other things. I truly feel undervalued and underpaid, in addition to a sort of simmering hostility. Oh, and the cost of my raise, I'm pretty sure, is about the same amount of money that she regularly snorts up her nose.

Over lunch she kept reiterating not how sorry she was, but "what a huge jump in pay it was," as if I had to apologize for seeking industry-standard pay. The more I type this out, the more angry I feel myself getting.

My initial reaction is to leave; however, after consideration, there aren't a ton of writing jobs in my area, less so for art. But I'm not sure I can stand it to stay. Any insight?

*Despondent and Disappointed*


## Dear Despondent,

DO YOURSELF a big favor. Leave this job. Find a job with paid time off, fixed hours and insurance. Write for yourself. Write what you have always wanted to write. Write on your own time. Form a writing group. Join a writing group. Form a small publication. Self-publish a book. Freelance. Do what you love.

But stay away from this toxic situation. This person lied to you and manipulated you. She induced you to give up something you wanted in return for something she promised but could not deliver.

Maybe she told herself she would deliver. Maybe she had no intention of delivering. Either way, she screwed you over. And she refused to admit it. She tried to sell you bullshit. It is destructive to work for a person like that.

So call the newspaper and see if it is still possible for you to work there. If there is no full-time position there, see about freelancing for the paper. And think big. Go directly for what you want. Start querying the big art magazines that you read. Develop story ideas. Use the contacts you have developed at this small, free arts paper to develop stories for bigger, more established magazines.

This has been my experience with small, arty publications run by needy, manipulative cokeheads who treat you like their nanny: You think you are giving up material satisfaction in exchange for some journalistic and artistic freedom. This can be true to an extent. You get access to the world of artists. It is interesting socially. It confers status. It opens doors. But needy, manipulative cokeheads will always screw you over. It's their nature.

> Greedy, manipulative cokeheads will always screw you over.

There are other problems too, ethical problems. If you find yourself developing an independent view that deviates from the commercial needs of the paper, your livelihood is in jeopardy.

General-interest newspapers are different. When you write about a traffic accident or a jury trial, there is no one advertising segment whose interests you are serving; your audience includes working people, teachers, students, business owners, professionals ... that broad, unruly mob we call the public. There are still difficult power relationships that influence what you can say without being fired for saying it. But the power is diffused.

I could say more but let's leave it at this:
Small, free arts paper run by cokehead?
Flee.

# I'm not afraid of writing, but I am afraid of publishing

*Some nameless fear stands between me and my desire to be heard.*

**Dear Cary,**

MAYBE IT'S FRUSTRATED writers week in your column, but reading the writer who didn't want to write compelled me to write. However, unlike that writer, I have no problems writing. I'm terrified of publishing.

To explain a bit about my situation—I've written my first novel. I'm quite proud of it. Although it's not perfect (does any writer think their work is ever completely "done"?) it does express something I find interesting, and if the feedback I've gotten from my writers group is any indication, others find it interesting too. Is it going to change the world of literature? No. I'd be very surprised, if I ever did publish it (a huge "if," I know), if more than a 100 people ever bought the book (and I'd largely suspect my family and friends of buying those first 100 copies).

The thought of publishing the novel terrifies me. However, I do long to be published. I would not be happy just writing for the sake of writing. I want to write to be heard. It's just that I'm afraid of being heard, as much as I want it.

I don't think it's the rejection that bothers me. I know publishing is a harsh business. But I've been rejected before and while painful (the sound of my ego crushing is never a pleasant thing), I know I can get over it. No, I'm truly terrified of success. I'm terrified of doing well. I'm not completely sure why. Maybe it's because I've had a series of jobs where I did well enough to get a paycheck but disliked the actual work I was doing and the thought of doing something I like is overwhelming. Maybe it's because I've idolized writers for so long that the thought of joining those ranks (maybe not in quality but just by sheer fact of publishing) is mind-boggling.

The thing is ... I don't get fearful very often. Rarely, in fact. I was never one of those people who got terrified about going to college (where I was an average student), or getting married, or moving a few hundred miles away from my family and friends for my spouse's career. So this becoming increasingly terrified of something I want is confusing me—both that it's happening and in figuring out how to cope with it.

Have any suggestions?

*A terrified would-be published writer*


## Dear Terrified,

I DON'T KNOW why you are reluctant to be published. I do have a couple of general beliefs about fear, and about writing. One is that when we say we are afraid of something, we may be using a general term to stand in for a specific but undiscovered— or unadmitted—object. To be afraid of "love," for instance, or "success" is to be afraid of particular things, including the emotions we might have, and the obligations we might incur, multifarious and varied and taxing. "Publishing" is not a discrete experience, but a collection of experiences. It is a life circumstance that creates many possibilities, both pleasant and unpleasant. So it is helpful to consider the object of our fear in detail, examining each component.

In our inner cinematic representation of "getting published," there is perhaps the early morning phone call from a mogul in New York. The mogul is standing at a window high above the city, looking out at the buildings at sunrise. Perhaps the mogul is wearing a cape. That would make it even better. The mogul tells us that our novel is being published, that it is a work of great distinction. The mogul thanks us for making the work.

That is not the moment you fear. It is perhaps some other moment—when you open a review and find the words "ill-conceived" and "banal" applied to your novel. When you read someone's public assessment of your writing ability as "minimal at best." Perhaps the reviewer, a stranger to you, even insults you personally or makes fun of you, inviting readers to laugh at a passage you thought was clever or touching. And maybe you see, suddenly, that he is right, and you feel as though you have been brought out on a brightly lit stage and exposed, accused and convicted. That is a moment to fear. There is also the fear of being invited into a crowded room where people you admire but have never met speak easily and knowledgeably to each other, laughing about matters you scarcely understand, and ask you for your opinion about a book you have not read. You have some half-chewed pâté in your mouth. It was spread thinly on a dry cracker. You are unable to say anything sparkling, and before you can finish chewing they have turned away. That is also a moment to fear.

These moments may happen. They have happened to many others. They are unpleasant. But they can be survived. For some writers, the fear of publishing would involve more threatening events: The writer might fear, with good reason, being shoved into a van and beaten, being put in prison and tortured, having his family murdered, being forced to sign a confession for crimes he did not commit. As weighed against the necessity of expressing yourself and being heard, your fears, whatever they are, are of minimal importance. Since you say you do not want to write just for yourself, that you want to be heard, there is only one choice for you: You must expose your work to the public. The way to do that is to submit it to publishers.

In doing so, you might consider my other general belief about fear—that it accompanies us through many necessary and desired tasks, like sweat, or flies. It is not something to base a decision on, any more than the rain is. It sometimes must simply be borne.

There is nothing you can do about it. You just continue. If your fear makes it difficult to submit your work to publishers, then you must find reinforcement for action: Make a schedule, commit to working with a friend, do the "Artist's Way," etc. There are many practical aids to accomplishing tasks that fear would otherwise prevent you from accomplishing.

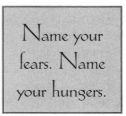

Name your fears. Name your hungers.

But writing and publishing are different things. They can be antithetical in their aims—one to gain self-knowledge, the other to gain power in the world. Although you say you want your voice to be heard, and though some may say that writing solely for oneself is pointless, I have grave misgivings about using writing as a way to make a living. I have discussed this elsewhere: Putting your writing to the service of supporting you economically can work against the true aims of your writing. If your writing, for instance, aims to deconstruct or obliterate the world, then to force your writing to please other people can be harmful to a process that for some reason is necessary for you, spiritually or emotionally or artistically. Perhaps you need to obliterate the world in order to discover obscure connections between things that are invisible to others. Perhaps you need to write incomprehensibly for a period of time. To write incomprehensibly may be helpful to you as a writer—to write gibberish, to free-associate. If we must always write only for the immediate comprehension of a broad cross section of people, then many possible expressions are eliminated from consideration. There may be times when you do not want to write for publication, but only for yourself, to discover something.

You don't have to publish. It's perfectly OK to write simply as a personal discipline; writing is fulfilling as a practice, like gardening. You may like to garden but not every gardener enters contests. I like to garden but I don't dream of making a living at it or showing my garden to people for their review and criticism. It's personal. It's my garden. I don't want to hear what you think about it. How can you disagree with a garden? It's a garden.

The garden shows me to myself. Writing shows you to yourself. It may be more valuable to you than to others. That's fine. People don't need to see you or me reflected back at them as much as they need to see themselves reflected back at them. If people would spend more time doing their own writing and reflection, and looking at how they themselves appear in words, they would probably be happier and acquire more self-knowledge, and we would be happier too, because they wouldn't be writing mean letters to us. Their own writing would be infinitely more valuable to them than our writing is. They'd be sitting, contemplating the way their own lives are reflected back at them in their daily writing, and they would see themselves in a new way, and possibly gain some compassion for themselves. They might also encounter some of the technical difficulties of making work that is accessible and meaningful to others, and thereby gain some measure of respect for the craft.

What is useful is to ask what "publishing" really means to you. Name your emotional hunger. Do you envision yourself on a stage receiving a prize, hearing speeches full of praise for your work, seeing the admiring faces? Do you envision the mogul in New York phoning you from an office high above Manhattan? Do you crave that? And what are your fears? Do you fear reading a negative review? Do you fear asking for an opinion and getting an uncomfortable silence? All these things are possible. But they can be borne. They are like the weather. So I urge you to name your fears. Name your hungers. Be exhaustive and specific.

And then do it anyway.

# I need more ideas! Where do they come from?

*I've been doing well selling my writing*
*but I seem to be running out of inspiration.*

## Dear Cary,

YOU SEEM TO have been answering a lot of questions from writers lately, but at the risk of annoying your nonwriting readership I'd like to ask another one. (At least this one extends to other professions as well.) Where do ideas come from? I seem to be out of them. I am a journalist with a specialized beat. I've been freelancing for close to two years. Scared of failing, I approached the first year with a lot of energy and ended up earning slightly more income than I'd ever made from the staff jobs I'd held. This last six months or so, though, I feel like I've lost steam. I'm still disciplined; I keep regular hours and never turn on the TV during the day. But my work volume is down, and I don't know how to turn it around. I write often for certain less prestigious publications for which I'm a regular contributor. Although they don't have newsstand flash, they pay well and the editors usually come to me with ideas that they know I'll be able to tackle well. Occasionally, I write for more prestigious publications that reach big audiences. I'd like to do more of that, but clearly these publications are not knocking at my door begging me to grace their pages with my words.

I need to convince them both that I can write and that I have ideas worth writing about. Every now and then I have a spark of brilliance and pitch a great idea that goes somewhere. But I need to be pitching weekly, not bimonthly, if I want my career to go anywhere. I read the breaking news, I take walks to clear my head, I browse at the library ... yet I seem stuck, unable to manufacture the bright, shiny new ideas that I need to compete. Am I just not an idea person? Or is there a way to become one?

*Thoughtless*

P.S. For the record, I know you're a fan of writers groups, but there don't seem to be any in my area, especially not targeting my particular specialty.

Dear Thoughtless,

ALTHOUGH I LOVE the question of where ideas come from, I think this is more about business performance and selling.

You already have what it takes. You are doing amazingly well. To go freelance and actually do better than you were doing on staff—that's amazing! To have done as well as you have, you must be quite good at selling already.

There are only so many ideas in news. You cannot manufacture news. You can only come up with so many angles. So I don't think you need more ideas. I think you need to sell the ideas that you have. You need to compete. News is a finite resource and many, many people have access to the same news.

Since you have done well so far, you are in a good position. Now you need to become an even better salesperson. You need to fine-tune your sales operation. You may need to gain a more sophisticated and detailed intelligence about the markets you are selling to and your competitors. You may need to learn how to respond quickly when one market suddenly contracts—how to take advantage of it instead of being thrown off by it. You may need to learn how to break into new markets, such as those lucrative, high-profile publications, and close tough deals.

So I suggest you seriously take this on as a business thing. Learn to be a salesman.

And learn it from people who know how to do it.

Buy some books and take some courses.

Don't try to learn it from me! I am the worst salesperson in the world. I can think this stuff up but I can't do it.

Heck, when I was freelancing, I had ideas! You should hear some of the ideas I had! But I was a freelance disaster, a half-mad surrealist masquerading as a journalist, playing a diabolical, self-defeating game for his own obscure purposes! I was terrible! I did not understand the market and the business, but, even worse, my own psychological needs got in the way. I was asking favors. Please, please will you let 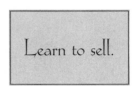 me write a piece for you? Will you please let me write in my strange, noncommercial way even though you are a commercial publication? Please will you risk your job and your standing among your colleagues to help me, even though there is no bond of trust between us? Because I'm special? Please?

That is not sales. That is begging. I was begging.

Anyway, I was not a salesperson.

You, on the other hand, are obviously doing it very, very well. You would not be making money as a freelancer if you were not already selling your ideas and your ability. So, again, I suggest you approach this as a coaching and learning opportunity. Move forward. Tweak the machine. Learn more about selling. Learn advanced selling techniques. Learn how to sell to the harder publications. Learn how to solve problems in sales. Learn how to close the deal.

How do you do that? I have no idea. But when you find out, let me know. I need to learn how to sell, too. And then, maybe we could sign up for the same course, and you could give me a ride? See, I have this book ... and this publishing business ... and these workshops ... and am organizing these creative getaways ... want to give me money? (See how bad I am?)

I should ask my life coach.

# How can I get a writing job?

*I'm a good writer. Everybody says so.*
*So how come other people get hired?*

Dear Cary,

THE ONLY THING I have ever wanted to do with my life was be a writer. Even when I was a little kid, that's what I told people I wanted to be when I grew up. Well ... here I am, very nearly a grown-up, and I'm still working shitty administrative assistant jobs. Everyone I know says I'm a talented writer and I'll get a great job one day; so then why do I know so many not-so-great writers who have great jobs? During college, I worked at my student newspaper, but I stuck to the copy desk and column writing because I was scared to interview people. Now, I'm willing to go interview people, but I can't get a job at a newspaper because I have no clips to show them. People tell me to get an internship as a way to get my foot in the door, but most internships are unpaid, and I can't afford to work for free. Often, I'll find a job online that I think I'm capable of, but I can't apply because they ask for multiple work samples and I have no reporting work to show them. Perhaps I could send them something from my blog or from my graduate thesis, but I doubt that's what they're looking for.

To make matters worse, a friend told me to apply for a specific job that she felt sure I could get, and now the editor has dropped off the planet for the past three weeks. It's just heart-wrenching when a job you thought had your name all over it vanishes into thin air. The thing that makes this so difficult is that I know I can write. I mean, really. I'm no Dostoevski, but I'm damned good, and I am absolutely 100 percent certain that, given the chance, I could make any newspaper or magazine proud. Now that I know it, how do I convince potential employers?

*Writer*

## Dear Writer,

THERE AREN'T ENOUGH writing jobs. There could be. It's not a natural law. If the government supported all writers, then there could be enough writing jobs. All you'd have to do is say, I am a writer, and the government would give you money for food and rent and say, "Bring me writing every day."

Then the government would have to figure out what to do with all the surplus writing. Maybe it would hand out the writing for free off the backs of trucks. But maybe no one would want all that surplus writing because it does not make a sandwich.

So then maybe the government would have to hire surplus readers who would be given money for food and rent and would go to the Big Surplus Writing Room where all the surplus writing was stacked on tables.

It could work that way. Every writer would be employed and read. I'm just saying.

But in our system writing must go into publications that people buy or that advertisers buy space in, or writers don't get money for food and rent.

So writers have to compete.

Competing is a whole separate thing from writing, but if you want to write for a living you have to compete. Look at all the other writers. They want the same thing.

You are competing for the attention and high regard of the person who decides.

So you say to the person who decides, Oh, yeah, that would be really funny, when they say, Wouldn't this be funny? Or if they say, Here's an idea, you say, I like that idea. That idea is a good idea. I would love to write about that idea.

And then they say, Yeah? You want to write this?

And you say, Absolutely.

Not everyone likes the person who says, That would be really funny. Some people like the writer who says, That sounds really dumb. They think that a writer who says, That would be really dumb must have a mind of her own.

But basically what they want is good stuff cheap from somebody who smells good. If you smell good and can give them good stuff cheap they might not like you but they like to get good stuff cheap. Not free. They'll think it's worthless. But cheap. Give them good stuff cheap. Smell good. They'll like that.

The other way is to do the work. If there is an interview do the interview. If the interview subject asks, What publication? say you're freelance. Don't say the name of the publication. The subject will call people at the publication and they will say they've never heard of you. Then it will seem like you made something up. They don't like that. They can be touchy. They think they're important. So be honest: You are freelance.

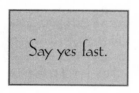

Say yes fast.

If you want the interview, be fun. That helps. Famous people who are bored like it if you are fun. They wanted life to be fun so they did fun things and got famous. So if you are fun they may agree to be interviewed by you even if the interview is not for sure going to get published. They might want to "give you a break." Some people are like that.

That way you get clips.

Also: Say yes fast. If the person who hires writers comes out of his cave and says, Who has 500 words on my mother's new play? do not pause to think, What is his mother's name, and what is her play, and is it that play that is not very good? Raise your hand and say, I, sir, have 750 words on your mother's new play, and might I add, sir: Brava!

Then they let you in the gate and the rest of the writers have to stand outside pretending to buy one another drinks. Once inside, you say, I completely lied, and then they beat you, but they are not very strong. They are editors.

That's one way. I'm just saying, you'll look around and you'll see writers saying completely untrue things to get work. And you'll think, those things are completely untrue, why are they saying them? They are saying them to get work. You say that certain books were flawed but interesting. What was interesting about them was their flaws.

You don't have to do this. There are other ways. You can be really, really good. You can find a niche. You can slog it out. But just don't be on your high horse. It's not like they're handing out rewards for talent. It's more like mud wrestling.

# I'm an artist going crazy in a dysfunctional magazine!

*There's no editor, the staff sleep at their desks, and we steal copyrighted material off the Internet!*

## Dear Cary,

I'M IN A quandary about my career. I currently work as an advertising designer for a tiny company that publishes a magazine. On paper, the job would seem to fit me well. It's in my career field (graphic design/journalism), no long hours, no mammoth corporate bureaucracy, and hey, I even get health insurance.

The problem is this: I have no respect for the people I work with and the company has no integrity. My co-workers can be found sleeping at their desks or surfing porn sites, the management is out shopping or at the spa, and sexual harassment is an everyday occurrence. Also, the magazine has no editor, and there's not even a pretense of journalistic integrity. We've gone so far as to copy and paste stories right off the Internet and publish them in the magazine in blatant violation of copyright laws. To sum it up, my workplace is a chaotic circus inhabited by incompetents.

The immediate question is this: Do I sit down, shut up and do as I'm told for the sake of a meager paycheck or look for greener pastures? And how do I avoid ending up in the same dysfunctional environment at a different company? This also raises deeper questions such as: Is it too much to expect for a job to be fulfilling or should just getting paid be enough?

I'm also caught in a repeating pattern of getting a job that seems well suited to me, initially enjoying the job, but then growing to hate it in a year's time. I don't have a particularly lengthy career history, but still long enough to see this pattern emerge. Ideally, I'd like to be self-employed as a fine artist, but given the odds against artists, I'm not willing to risk homelessness in pursuit of my art. Any advice would be greatly appreciated.

*Future Postal Worker*

## Dear Future Postal Worker,

SO YOUR CO-WORKERS are sleeping at their desks and surfing porn sites, the management is out shopping or at the spa, and sexual harassment is an everyday occurrence?

Are you sure you don't work at Salon?

Seriously, it is time to look for greener pastures. It shouldn't be hard to find greener pastures, actually. Your case is pretty rare. In fact, I doubt you could easily find another magazine this strange and dysfunctional. Even the worst magazines have editors, or at least people who call themselves editors when they fire you. It sounds like what you're working for is some kind of criminal front rather than an actual magazine. I would get out of there.

Publishing attracts the crazies. Some are crazy and well-meaning. Some are just crazy. There's usually some strange economic arrangements whereby, for instance, instead of a paycheck management offers you free dental work. You notice the publisher's new scarily white teeth. Your new assignment is to interview the proprietor of Mister ShinyTeeth Cosmetic Dentistry and Bikini Waxing, and soon it's, You know, this job just is not a good fit.

The larger question you raise is about how to live one's life as an artist. That's the big question.

While everyone who is called to be an artist is different, I think certain general things can be said about the practical problem of finding time and space in life to pursue art.

First of all, it's not optional. If you are an artist, you are called. Ignoring your desire to make art is not possible. That will only kill you. You must make a choice as to how to make art. You must consciously decide how to marshal your material resources to meet your spiritual needs.

One choice is to take the plunge and determine to make your art and live on it, come what may. You find the cheapest place you can find where there is space for you to work. You minimize all your expenses. You strip down your life to the essentials. You figure out what it costs to eat and clothe yourself and you get to work. You don't spend money on anything except what it takes to survive and do your work. Either you have money saved or you sell pieces or you have a part-time job that does not require you to think about anything, so you just show up and do your job and then go home and do your art. This is not complicated but neither is it easy. Our desires are many, as are the lures of pleasure and entertainment and comfort. But it can be done. You are free to do this. I encourage you to try it if it appeals to you, and if it doesn't work, if it is too harsh an existence, then you are free to stop doing it and find something more comfortable.

> Publishing attracts the crazies.

The other option, which is more comfortable, is to take a gradualist approach. Find a job or an area of work that is not too taxing, and make for yourself a space where you can work on your art an hour or three a day, and on weekends. Work steadily over the years. Sell work as you can. Make friendships and be a part of an arts community. Take classes. Practice. Study. Get better. Keep at it. Use your art as a vehicle to know yourself. Eventually you may reach a point where you can support yourself on your art, or you may not. But you have a sustainable life that includes art even though it may not be completely about art.

Some artists find that, if they must have a job, it is better to have a job not in their field. The problem with having a job in your field is that all your creative powers may be brought to bear in your job. Whereas if you are flipping burgers or something, you may be free to save up all your creative energy for your artwork.

In either case, the important thing is to start now. The worst thing to do is to drift, thinking that one day soon you will settle down and get to work on your craft in some way. Decide today whether you are going to go for broke or try to build a sustainable long-term life that includes art.

This is a serious matter. You must do something. Experiment. Find something that works for you. Seek support from others. Be kind to yourself. Do not despair. Keep at it. Make a life of it.

And stay out of dysfunctional magazines.

.

# I'm doing stand-up and it's working. Should I quit my job?

*I don't want to blow an opportunity, but I don't want to end up in the gutter either. What's my choice?*

**Dear Cary,**

I'M A SINGLE woman in my late 30s. I have a white-collar job that is not exciting, but pays decently with good benefits and lots of security. I could be way worse off. A few years ago I started doing stand-up comedy at open mics around town. Guess what? I don't suck! I've had my share of bad sets and certainly bombed a few times, but I've also had a good number of great sets, and even some killer ones. Considering the relatively short time I've been doing stand-up, I'm progressing quite nicely.

Winning over a roomful of strangers who moments ago didn't give a shit about you, getting laughs from an original joke that you wrote, having veteran comics congratulate you on your set ... it's a great feeling. Being a comic has become part of my identity—I'm not just another office drone. Stand-up is an arena where I don't have to play nice, fit in and keep a low profile. I can be clever, snide, dirty and raw. When you make them laugh, nobody minds that you are the smartest person in the room. And it's impossible not to wonder just how far I could go as a comic. Fame? Money? Could I get all that? Here's my problem: The late nights are killing me. Stand-up requires spending many nights hanging out in divey bars

86

waiting for your turn at the mic, and networking with other comics and MCs. This is not compatible with keeping up appearances at a 9-to-5. It also doesn't fit in well going to the gym and doing my other hobbies and interests. Like anything else, stand-up requires a consistent effort in order to become truly proficient. You can't do it half-assed. I feel like my options are: 1) become an overweight, single-minded, exhausted, miserable person but a really great comic or 2) become a fit, well-rounded person who would be quite emotionally healthy if it weren't for that whole gave-up-on-a-dream thing.

What do you think, Cary?

*Not a Hack*

## Dear Not a Hack,

FROM PERSONAL EXPERIENCE I can say that if you continue as you are, something will break. You will crack up or get sick. You will blow a big gig or you will blow off your job or you will find yourself strangely drawn to momentary ecstasies that blur your vision.

So if you are smart (Don't look at me! I had to learn from experience!) you will begin now to look for a new job. The new job will be flexible. It will allow you to come in late and work from home when necessary. It will allow you to take time off on short notice. It may not pay as well as the current job or be as secure, but it will allow you to keep doing the stand-up.

Your goal will be to gradually increase the income from the stand-up and become less dependent on the straight job. What you want to do is decrease the time and energy you spend on the straight job, and expand your dramatic activities—expand your writing, prepare parts for movies, try writing scripts, take acting workshops, audition for plays and movies, etc.

It's not either/or. It's both. You take care of business and you do your art. You play roles. In your art maybe you act crazy. But in your life, you play the adult role. You act smart. You arrange things. You take care of your art.

Your art doesn't know what the fuck it's doing. It's art. What does it know? Your art is like a kid. You have to be the parent and take care of it. It's a big job. Some people get this intuitively. Others, like me and perhaps like you, we have to figure it out. It takes work.

I used to think books like *The Artist's Way* and some such were for sissies. I had this macho view of being an artist: If you are an artist, you are stronger than everyone else. You just do it. You don't need no stinkin' *Artist's Way.* You don't need no stinkin' help. Help is for sissies. Real artists just work and work and work. But now I see that while you, the adult, may not need help, your art does. It needs all the help it can get.

> Your art is like a kid. You have to be the parent and take care of it.

I had this notion that real artists don't think and plan. That was a very crazy notion. It arose out of a misreading of the romantic tradition and the tradition of inspiration and spontaneity.

The truth is that thinking and planning are very difficult and they require courage and serenity. But they are essential to creativity. One may be greatly talented but lack life management skills. There is no shame in that. One can acquire life management skills more easily than one can acquire the ability to make people laugh.

Failure is not funny or artistic. It's just failure. So don't fail. Get the resources you need. Set up an ongoing survival structure. Do you need occasional counseling and psychotherapy? Look into it. Do you need financial planning? Look into it. Do you need accounting services, housekeeping, pet sitting, wardrobe? Look into the necessary maintenance services. Set yourself up as a going concern. And then keep going.

I'm in it for the long haul now. Let's all be in it for the long haul. Let's survive. There is much, much, much more to do. It's a very interesting world, and a very funny world, too. Let's survive.

# I'm a jazz pianist, nearly 50, and I need to make some real money!

*I can't believe how little one makes practicing "America's only original art form."*

Hi, Cary,

I'M APPROACHING 50 years old. I've been a jazz pianist for nearly 30 years. I'm not anyone you've ever heard of. I'm good but not great. I never thought I would be famous, and that doesn't bother me. I've had lots of hotel and restaurant gigs, accompanied hundreds of lame wannabe singers (and some good ones, too) and done thousands of gigs in jazz clubs, some with incredible musicians and some where nobody was listening. I always thought if I stuck with it, I'd be able to make a living. I think I read somewhere that the average jazz musician these days makes about $17,000 a year. A 50-year-old making that seems pathetic. I do better than that, but not by much. I've spent my life climbing this ladder of musical success and found out when I got near the top that the ladder was against the wrong wall. I'm not married and don't have kids. Never would have been able to afford them. That would have been nice.

How can a person like me change into something different? It seems impossible and I don't know where to begin.

We always hear heart-warming stories of people who followed their dream and never gave up and so forth, but what of the people who followed their dream and failed? We don't want to hear about them.

I'm an intelligent person. I have two master's degrees. One in music, the other in fine arts (another useful degree). Yet I have absolutely no idea about how to go about making money.

Yes, that is what I want. Money. I want health insurance. I want a decent place to live. I want to think maybe I won't have to be taking lousy gigs at age 80 to buy a meal.

I don't think I've been totally naive. I didn't strive for fame, à la "American Idol." I studied hard. I know music theory inside out. I checked out the history of jazz piano from Jelly Roll Morton to Keith Jarrett. I thought being true to your art was satisfaction enough. I guess it's not. I want the satisfaction of making a decent living. I'm tired of taking every $100 gig that comes my way to play for a tone-deaf singer. After I drive an hour each way, and pay the IRS its cut, and I end up with $50. This is what practitioners of "America's only original art form" have to deal with.

I really think I could leave it all behind. I could be happy playing the occasional gig for fun. Or playing for myself and friends. I'd like to do some more composing just for self-satisfaction. But I have no idea how to make a living! This revelation just drives me nuts. The thought of starting from scratch at my age is mind-boggling.

I know these questions are very broad. Most people look at me and think I'm lucky, that playing music for a living must be great. Other people in other occupations must feel the same. I'm just barely making a living. Is it possible for me to change?

*Musically Frustrated*


## Dear Musically Frustrated,

I, TOO, WAS frustrated this morning when I sat down to answer your letter. Nothing was coming. I went to the regular place where I go to get words and there were no words there.

Weird. Am I running out? I had to leave my house and walk around. I went to a meeting of the type I often attend. It was somewhat comforting but did not really help.

Then, standing on the street corner waiting for a train, I noticed a bumper sticker on an old Toyota Camry sedan. It said "Real musicians have day jobs!"

I felt that my prayers had been answered—yours too, actually.

It was a needed reminder: Your music does not have to support you. In fact, your music might be happier if you were supporting it.

You have done the almost impossible by supporting yourself as a jazz pianist all these years. It is a remarkable, heroic and admirable feat. That doesn't mean that at a certain point you can't sit out a few sets.

> Augment your income with related activities.

You may find it hard to change; deep down you may feel that what you are is a musician, end of story.

I felt at one time that I was a writer, end of story. But it wasn't end of story. Was more like beginning of story.

I did not gain freedom to write with fluidity and ease until I stopped believing that I had to be a writer.

I mean this in a big way. The import of it stems from the power and the invisibility of my belief that I did indeed have to be a writer. I had to! I believed not only that I had to be a writer, but also that I was my writing. I thought this stuff I put on paper was me. Literally. I thought it was me. At the same time, I did not know that this was what I thought until I heard myself saying "Yes, of course I am my writing!" But I learned, after some work with a helpful therapist, to see myself as a person who plays many roles. Yes, I write, but I also am a husband, a homeowner, a friend, a family member. I am also a person who deserves to take a rest now and then. I was killing myself trying to prove this hypothesis every day: I am a writer, end of story.

It's not the end of the story. It's more like the beginning of the story.

You sound like you are ready to make some changes.

What I suggest, again speaking from personal experience, is that you make some adjustments, but avoid making a sudden, cataclysmic break. Instead, first try augmenting your income with related activities. Create new but related income streams to incrementally improve your income: Sell a few CDs at gigs. Teach a class or two. Repair instruments now and then. Do a little booking. Do some engineering or production. Consult with club owners. And also make yourself useful in ways without demanding payment. Use some of your knowledge about the booking scene and find out how valuable your knowledge and your contacts are. When you see that your Rolodex, for instance, is valuable, think about ways you might use it, for booking or publicity. With your many contacts and your experience, you have valuable knowledge.

But again, my advice: Do this gradually. Do a little of everything. You may discover in this way that one of the ancillary activities seems to be the right model for a career change. If so, transition into it. But start small. Pay attention to percentages at first, not dollar amounts. If you can increase your income from one gig by 10 percent, consider that a victory. If you're only netting $50 on a gig, selling even two CDs at a $5 profit each is an increase of 20 percent for the night. If you keep your expenses at their current level and increase your income, your situation will start to improve.

At the same time, think about major changes. Maybe you will find that you really want to go into a totally new field. You could go into law or finance. It's not too late. You could do that. You could make major changes in the next year or two. But for now I think it is better to move gradually, using what you already have. And keep your eyes open for a new career that attracts you.

Over the weekend I found myself rereading *Straight Life*, the Art Pepper story. That guy had a hard life. He was out boosting construction tools from building sites in L.A. with his poodle named Bijou! To feed his heroin habit. And he's not alone. So many jazz musicians have died early deaths because it is so hard to be an artist and maintain sanity.

At least you don't have a heroin habit. (You don't have a heroin habit, do you? You couldn't have a heroin habit. You wouldn't be writing to me if you had a heroin habit!)

So congratulations! You have done well to keep yourself healthy all these years. You are an asset to our culture. You ought to be rewarded. But it is terrible what musicians have to go through. We ought to take better care of musicians. It's a terribly hard life.

So you're going to make a change. That's clear. You can teach. You can repair. You can do sales. You can get into booking. You can do engineering and production. You can do sound for movies.

All these things you can do without really a whole lot of extra education. You could learn on the job. And you can keep playing music while you make these changes.

Good luck. I'd like to say more, but I have a deadline, which is sort of like going onstage. You go up there with whatever you've got.

# Citizens of the Dream:

# Entanglements, Obligations and the Soul of the Artist

# My husband supported me in my art—should I now support him?

*I'm not the only creative one in the marriage;*
*I feel bad that he works a day job.*

## Dear Cary,

SEVERAL YEARS AGO, I did what a lot of people just dream about: I got to begin, and sustain, a career as a writer. I worked hard; I'd climbed out of a stifling marriage with a young child in tow and recognized that my midlife crisis wasn't going to be about a convertible or an ashram. It was never about the money (anyone who writes knows that already; note to everyone else: It can't be about the money), but I had responsibilities to my daughter that made total freedom to chase the dream ridiculous.

So, how did it come about? I met a lovely man a couple of years after the divorce. We are compatible; my daughter adores him; he is kind. He, too, was at a crossroads in his working life, and together we navigated a direction for him to become financially stable. I financially supported him through that time (several years) in my previous soul-sucking-but-sound job. When that was accomplished, I took my turn. I couldn't have done it without him.

The problem? He too is an artist. He's very good. He too has dreams. He works at his stable, unionized job (no, not the auto industry), which has great benefits and a pension. He worked hard to get there; but it's not what he craves. My question? Do I owe him the same chance that I got? I don't earn enough for him to quit his job. And in this economic climate, that would be crazy, whether he was with me or not.

He doesn't complain and is proud of my accomplishments. I have encouraged him to work on his art in his down time—which he instead uses to mostly watch TV or play games. I worry he's lost his ambition, while I'm recognizing mine. I work very hard in a very tight industry. I guess I don't know if he just doesn't have the ambition, or if I'm an albatross around his neck.

*Do I have a debt here?*


## Dear Possible Debtor,

YOU ASK IF you have a debt here. Apparently you feel a debt. You are uncomfortable. But do you owe a debt? I do not think so, just based on what you have said. What is given in love is freely given, and no one can go into debt by receiving what is freely given.

But you would like to see your husband pursue his art. You worry that you are in some way responsible for his success or failure. It bothers you that he does not use his time off work to pursue it. You worry that you are a burden.

What are you feeling, exactly? Are you mistaking gratitude for indebtedness? With gratitude comes a desire to repay. We do say things out of gratitude; we imagine repaying the favor. In doing so, we sometimes create indebtedness where before there was only gratitude. Sometimes we do this because, on a deeper level, we are unable to truly receive. We are controlling what comes our way; we rob an individual of the power to give. We take what is given as if it were a loan.

That is somewhat theoretical and idealistic. In marriage we also make deals. It is possible that, explicit or not, you and he have some sort of understanding. That is what you need to figure out: not whether you feel indebted, but whether you and he had some agreement.

Did you say to him at some point, "One day I will repay the favor"?

It's possible that you did.

What has passed between you? Is there something lurking underneath, some expectation that could turn to grinding resentment if not acknowledged? And what of the creative urge itself? That alone, if not answered, can turn sour.

Whether you "owe" him or not, there are things you can do. You can help him enroll in some classes or workshops. You could perhaps get him a workshop session as a gift.

> We do not owe back what is freely given.

But despite all that, in the matter of creativity, whatever debt is owed to his creative self only he can pay. Only he can nurture his own creative self. If he is wasting it or squandering it or strangling it or ignoring its calls, he can be nudged toward it, or put in a position to hear it, but he is going to have to do the nurturing. Let's hope he does.

It is hard to conjure up inspiration in our art after working a job all day. But a workshop can at least put him in touch with his materials. Often that is all that is needed to stimulate creativity. We sometimes think that a feeling of inspiration should precede our activity, but it works the other way. Sit down and begin playing notes and you may soon be making up a song. Sit down and start putting words on paper, or typing them on the screen. Soon the words will add up; a verbal artifact will take shape.

Witness this moment: Having dithered all week, I finally, on deadline, sit down and finish something.

# Should I move to the city for my art?

*I'm sick of this two-bit town, my loafer
boyfriend and my dull cubicle job.*

**Dear Cary,**

I REALLY ENJOY your writing, turning problems into art. I have
long wanted to write you, but my troubles are so broad—abusive
childhood and all of its aftereffects; self-destructive behavior,
depression and debt. I write run-on sentences (also, surely, a
byproduct of a troubled past). I am doing what one ought to, trying not to self-destruct, seeing a therapist and taking some meds.
I have often been lonely, moving from place to place. I do have
friends; I tend to make them wherever I go, though I have trouble
internalizing their affection. I married a nice man and then I got
bored and left him. I have high highs and very low lows, but have
always had my art to keep me going.

I am now 33 and have been in a loving, passionate and very
absorbing relationship for five years. He is a bit of a ne'er-do-
well, but he makes me laugh and he certainly loves me in spite of
my issues, which you can imagine are not few. I have been supporting us financially the past year with my soul-draining 9-to-5
job, working in my studio whenever I can. He has not been doing
anything, but he is seeing a therapist about this very fact (possible attention deficit disorder). Though this past year was difficult, we have been happy together in our small town. I, however,
can't face another year of things being the same, the meaningless

toil without any progress made in my career as an artist. I can't go on sitting in a cube in a town with so little opportunity. So I am off to the big city, and my sweetheart is very supportive of my leaving. He is also not coming with me, because he has a child (age 7) who lives nearby with his ex. I can't argue with that reason, but I suspect he wouldn't come anyway, as he is intimidated by the idea of living anywhere besides the familiar old town.

I feel angry and disappointed at having to make this choice, because he is supposed to be the love of my life, and it certainly feels that way, so how can he let me go? I guess this is unfair, since I am the one leaving, and yet I feel sad and jealous to see all of my other friends traveling in pairs, going along for the journey. I am otherwise excited (and also nervous) about the big change and the opportunities the big city affords, but this is a pretty big otherwise. I am upset that he will not be there to support me after all this time invested, that I have to go it alone.

He seems to think that if we frame the situation more positively, it does not have to be the end for us. We can simply decide that we are still a couple, and conduct a long-distance relationship for as long as it takes. Of course, I would have to return for us to reunite, as he says he would never consider joining me there.

There are definitely some benefits to us spending some time apart. I would like to focus my time on my work after being so absorbed in our relationship these last few years, and without me he has a chance to be self-sufficient and (I hope) begin to engage himself in all of the projects that until now he has only dreamed about. I don't want to end this relationship, having had so little love in my life until now, but I wonder if it is silly to think I can keep it going for an indefinite period of our no longer living together. What can I do to improve our chances? I feel a sad kind of distance already forming, but this is probably just me, framing things as negatively as possible, as I am wont to do. Should I try one last time to convince him that a four-hour drive/train/bus ride from his kiddo is not the end of the world, or is that selfish and ridiculous? How do I get Mr. Optimism to see the very real threat of this situation (if there is one)? Would it make a difference if I could? Am I inventing this whole problem?

I can choose how to feel about this whole thing to some extent, and I can definitely choose my actions, but I wonder what is wise or realistic. My train doesn't leave for a few months, and I wonder what I should spend this time doing as far as my darling is concerned. Probably not alternately obsessing and moping. Or getting mad.

*Self-Fulfilling Prophet*

## Dear Self-Fulfilling,

MY ADVICE WOULD be to do some more thinking about this choice.

You say it yourself: You do have friends, but you have trouble internalizing their affection. You move from place to place. You have self-destructive behavior. On the surface, it appears you're about to manifest all of that right in front of our eyes.

Presumably you are in therapy to change the behavior that has caused you so much trouble in the past. The first step in changing that is to recognize what it is. You've gotten that far. I think now you have to take the next step and try to do things differently this time.

Hard as it may be, and as unsatisfying, I think you need to take stock of what you have, all the satisfactions of your deadbeat boyfriend and your studio, your friends, your knowledge of the town. Do that first, at least. Make a good-faith effort. And see what you can do to fix things up a little. All you really want is a job that pays the bills, right? You're not on some big career path, are you? You want to be an artist. So you need more time to work on your art. That means a different job, but not necessarily a fancy exciting job. Maybe a job with a window. Just get a job where you can look out the window a lot. Find a job that is really dumb. Conserve your energy and your rage. Spend more time in your studio. And tell your boyfriend you can't support him anymore. You can't afford it. If you're going to do your art you need somebody who can pay his own way. He sounds wonderful. But if you can't afford him, you can't afford him. Tell him he's going to have to come up with some cash.

And what about the big city? What exactly is there that you are looking for? If you had studio space, a place to live and gallery representation I could understand it. Or if you were planning to go to art school I could understand that. But what opportunities does the big city afford if what you really want is more time to work on your art? It's usually more expensive to live in a big city and you have to spend more of your time making money to survive. Plus studio space is more expensive.

It is true that cities are where they keep the art. But if you want to absorb the art of the city, then why not make the four-hour trip to the city to see the art? That way it's an adventure.

Also, I think there is something about traveling specifically to see art that focuses the mind. Ask people who live in a city how often they go to the museums and galleries. For most of them, not often enough.

> Build on what you have, where you are.

So I seriously think you should reconsider. You've got a good thing right now where you are. You have issues of abuse that you're making good progress with. Throwing away all the support and stability you have could be more unsettling than you realize. Making a big change could cause more problems to resurface.

But maybe when you reconsider you will in the end find that your spirit longs for the city and that's that. If so, at least you will have done more work on the practical side. And if it is indeed not your spirit per se, but just the spirit of "fuck this," then perhaps I will have saved you a lot of grief and heartache.

Either way, I commend you on your journey!

# My sister is a famous designer—and I'm not!

*I do good work but I fear I'm mediocre,
and my heart is poisoned with jealousy.*

Cary,

BY MANY MEASURES, I am a successful designer. I live in a beautiful home, take my daughters on wonderful vacations, have some money put away for retirement. This is colored by the fact that my sister is in the same business as me but has become rich at it. In fact, she is famous. In fact, you unquestionably know her work and probably make use of the products she has designed in your home. You may have been peripherally aware of mine, but you have not bought them or admired them. My daughters say nice things about my designs. They go wild over their aunt's. Just tonight I learned that she has made a hugely lucrative deal for a new line of brilliant designs.

None of this is the real problem. The real problem is that she is a great artist, and I am a smart gal who works hard, knows how to sell herself, and comes up with some good but ultimately forgettable stuff once in a while, and I can not look at this in any way that does not cause me pain. Maybe if I were rich, too, and could tell the business I am in to go to hell, I would feel differently. But I need to stay in the game. My husband and I are not set up for me to cash out yet. And at this point in my life I wouldn't be hireable doing anything else, and certainly nothing else that would keep me in the lifestyle that my family and I enjoy. Plus for all its frustrations it's a great life, being in this business. The problem is the constant sense that I'm just not good enough, not the artist I wanted to be, and not the artist my sister is. This has poisoned my life for many, many years. Cognitive therapy has helped a little but only temporarily. My sister and I are very close, and our relationship is not poisoned by my jealousy—just my heart.

I'll go a step further here. If I took my sister out of the picture, I would still be disappointed with my work. Forgettable, minor, only OK. I would still be unhappy about it. Even as I work at it day after day.

My husband tells me again and again that we have a wonderful life and that I shouldn't suffer over this. I love that he says it, but I don't feel it.

Do you have any words of enlightenment that might help me get to where this is not such a big part of my thinking and my life? Where I do not feel an emptiness where pride and satisfaction in my work should be? Where reading about sister's latest triumph doesn't lay me out for a day?

Thanks,

*The Younger and Less Talented Sister*


## Dear Younger and Less Talented Sister,

STOP BEATING YOURSELF up! Jesus! Just stop it!

Come on, now. You have to fight your way out of this. You have to fight this bitchy, killing voice. Get mad at it. Fight back. Tell it to go fuck itself. Banish it. Get it out of your head. It doesn't belong there.

Replace it with something good: You are a talented artist. You are a talented artist you are a talented artist you are a talented artist!

The minute you hear that voice in your head that says you've wasted your life doing mediocre design, stop it. Don't do it. When you start to do it, stop as soon as you realize what you're doing. Say out loud, I am a designer. I am an artist. I make honest work. I make a living at my work! I'm a good designer. I do good work!

Just like you, I fucking beat myself up night and day until I'm black and blue because I'm not the guy who wrote *The Corrections* even though I couldn't even read *The Corrections*, and I couldn't even read *A Heartbreaking Work of Staggering Genius* even though I'd like to be Dave Eggers, and why the fuck would I want to be Dave Eggers? Because I'm a sick fucker, that's why, because I hate myself. And I have to stop doing that. I have to love myself.

I have to love myself because loving myself is the only thing that stands between me and suicide.

I love myself because I have to. I love myself because suicide is not an option. I love myself because other people love me and I've got no right. So I love myself immoderately and without delay. I love myself without recompense, without reason, without state sponsorship or licensing, without writing a proposal first or getting a grant, without getting dressed up first and taking a shower, without calling ahead to find out what time I should love myself, without buying a bottle of wine and some flowers first, without shining my shoes and clipping my nails. I love myself because of you. I love myself because there are people like you and me all over the world beating ourselves up because our sisters made more money, because our sisters are more perfect, because everybody loves our sister better. Jesus, woman! Love yourself! Take the afternoon off. Pick up something you've made that you love and admire it. Spend all day admiring it. Don't criticize it. Don't pick it apart. You made it. You are a creative person. You don't control the market. You don't even control your creativity. It's a gift. Take care of it.

Love yourself because you've got no choice. It's that or end up in an institution where they hand you your meds in a little cup from a window.

I know I'm not Dostoevski or even Paddy Chayefski. I'm a guy with a mortgage and hungry dogs. So I love myself because I have to, because the alternative is not an option. I talk to God unabashedly and say what's up, you fucker, what fresh hell have you so graciously arranged for me today? I bless myself. I say bless you, fuckhead, bless you, my son, let's see you make it through this day without driving off a cliff. Let's see you smile in line at the grocery store and try to make small talk with the cashier. Let's see you ride all the way from here to the ocean with murderous voices murmuring in your skull. Good morning, fuckhead, bless you for another day. What do you think this is, the Ritz?

The murderous voice says do you, Cary Tennis, take this life to be your lawful welded life and I say, I do. And do you, life, take this man to be your impoverished and humble obedient slave, to breath in and out until God knows what unholy combination of stress, disease, cell mutations, poison, decay and entropy force him finally into one last dark half-breath? And life says, Yeah, sure, why not. And so we go on, me and my weary bride of life, two ragged beggars hiding behind the Safeway looking for cans and cigarette butts.

> You are a talented artist. Now get back to work.

Oh, I don't know, I do exaggerate. I have a good if perilous middle-class existence. And so do you. But in our hearts, if we are artists, we are hungry and desperate. That is utterly normal. That is our condition. That is the condition of the creative person, to be hungry and desperate without moderation. Our job is to continue in our crazy journey with immoderate and unearned joy in our hearts and keep creating things, immoderately and without delay, desperately, beyond all reason.

But let's talk reasonably here just for a minute before I jump off a cliff. Why did cognitive therapy help only temporarily? Is that because you only practiced it temporarily? Are you practicing it now? Are you using the tools that got you some relief? You have to do it every day. If you've stopped doing it and it's not working, it's not working because you're not doing it. So start doing it again. If you're using cognitive therapy but it isn't working enough, work at it harder. It worked once. It worked because it's effective. But the dysfunctional voices of self-hatred and despair will happily come back. So you have to keep doing it. You have to keep them at bay. It's a maintenance thing. So keep working it.

Don't let these stupid voices in. Don't give them a chance. Kill them unmercifully. Do cognitive therapy every day until it hurts. Do what works. Do it till it hurts.

And don't idolize your fucking sister so much. She's a designer just like you.

OK. Enough of this.

Now get back to work.

# My husband shuts me down when I mention fine arts grad school

*I put my arts education on hold for work and family. Now I'm feeling a powerful pull.*

**Dear Cary,**

I EARNED A bachelor's degree in fine art 11 years ago. I was a good student, and intended for a while to go to graduate school, just not immediately. A year or so after graduating, I got married. This was followed by the adventure of self-employment (my husband and I working together as entrepreneurs), then two children (and No. 3 is on the way).

During these almost 10 years of marriage, I have managed to do a little here and there with my artwork. I've exhibited a couple of times in small galleries and I received a grant once, but it's not much to write home about and it's spread out over many years. Over the past year and a half, I have had some breakthroughs, and am now producing more and better art than I have in a long time. I've exhibited twice in our small town, with positive feedback. I am finally getting on track with balancing the family stuff and being true to myself. I am even pretty confident that having another baby won't disable my momentum entirely.

So here's the dilemma. I still would really like to go to graduate school. I think a lot of my reasons for it are somewhat emotional, or at least not necessarily entirely rational, but I still want it. My husband, on the other hand, does not think it's a good idea at all. I've brought it up to him occasionally over the years, and always got shot down. Though he's by far the most intelligent man I've ever met, he chose not to go to college. He says he isn't against higher education in general, and would probably want our children to go. But he just shuts me down when I bring up the idea.

We're currently contemplating a move to a new city, primarily for business reasons. This new city happens to have a very appealing university with just the right master's program for me. I looked over their information and I really think I could get into the program in a year or so. He feels that in the field I'm working in I should just continue with what I'm doing, i.e., paint as much as possible and try to get gallery shows whenever I can, to build up a résumé.

He makes some good points. It's not like this is medicine or law or something that you simply can't do without a degree. And I do have a bachelor's already. How helpful is an MFA to the career of a fine artist anyway? Part of me sure thinks it would be helpful, both for the education itself, and because having that credential boosts you in the eyes of curators.

So if I'm right, and grad school would be beneficial, how do I go about convincing him? It's not the kind of thing I could do without his agreement. Where we left it after our last conversation on the subject was that I still wanted it, and if I found ways of articulating why I found it valuable I'd bring it up again. In the meantime I'd stay the course and work sans degree, which is what I should be doing to prepare for school anyway.

I could probably make a go of it and be satisfied with the degree I have. I've just always put a very high value on academia, and being told basically that I can't go just grates on me. I think I'd get accepted, and I think it would cost little to nothing with all the stipends grad students get. Does this seem like a sensible goal, and if so how do I convince my husband?

*Needing Justification*

## Dear Needing Justification,

I FIND IT troubling that your husband will not support you in your desire to go to graduate school in fine arts unless you can demonstrate why it is beneficial. And you don't just say he disagrees with you. You say he shuts you down.

Why would he want to shut you down?

Sometimes things are valuable to us in ways we cannot articulate. One of the benefits of being married to a sympathetic and compatible person is that they will support us in our quest even when we cannot articulate what it is we are searching for or why it is valuable. This is particularly important for creative people. Creative people must be allowed to follow their hungers; sometimes they have nothing else to go on.

It is possible that your husband is indeed highly intelligent but does not understand this. If he cannot see, on his own, why further schooling is important to you then perhaps he simply lacks insight into your nature. If he lacks insight, that is unfortunate for him— but his shortcoming should not be allowed to interfere with your creative life. Perhaps he sees your artistic career as just another kind of business, one that has no bearing on education. He may not understand that for you, the education is an end in itself.

I suspect there is also an emotional component that he has not revealed. Perhaps your desire to go to graduate school strikes him like a desire for flight. Perhaps he would prefer that you stay on the ground with him, tending to the business. Perhaps he feels that he already spends all his time on the ground while you roar about in the sky with the crowd below waving up at you in admiration. (He stands in the shadow of the hangar, greasy in his jumpsuit, holding a wrench, bitterly watching, wishing you would shut it down and land.)

But if he has certain feelings of that nature, he ought to lay them on the table. That's the decent thing to do. As it is, he is being rather cunning and controlling. On the surface, he seems to be making a reasonable request: "Explain to me, make me understand." And yet he is actually proposing an impossible task, one in which you undoubtedly will fail. For how can you reliably demonstrate the future practical benefits of a fine arts education?

If every artist were required to articulate what concrete benefits he or she will gain before embarking on further education, the arts would be in serious trouble. Sometimes hunger is the artist's only compass.

However, I know this is not the kind of argument likely to gain favor with a pragmatic, realistic sort of person. So if you are interested in trying to make a rational argument, there are a couple.

> Sometimes hunger is your only compass.

One is a sort of macroeconomic audit of the emotional Zeitgeist: You could argue that the costs and benefits of the two choices are widely asymmetrical. That is, if you do not go, you will be seriously deprived of great personal benefits, while your husband receives no particular benefit. But the reverse is not true. If you do go, you will receive great personal benefits, while your husband is not seriously deprived. He may be inconvenienced, but he will not be deprived of his dream. Therefore, the costs to the emotional Zeitgeist are greater if you do not go than if you go.

There is another argument, closer to the ground, which is simply that school is a good social investment. It increases one's status and credibility. It opens doors. It brands you as serious. It has a whole host of socioeconomic benefits that you could probably back up with research.

But arguing with him on his own terms may only lead to failure. If you say "macroeconomic audit of the emotional Zeitgeist" he will probably burst out laughing and ask you where you got that nonsense. And it is nonsense, in a way: The simple truth is that you're an artist and you feel the need to go for more education and that should be enough right there. What you are craving is not a pragmatic thing, not a product, but a kind of experience, a way of being that cannot be quantified or monetized. You're an artist. End of story.

So I would say simply that if he wants you to be happy as an artist, he must allow you to make your own decisions about your artistic career. And whatever effect that has on the family and the family business you will just have to deal with.

# I live in a secret fantasy world

*I'm a mom with three kids, but in my mind
I'm a princess, a genius and a famous writer.*

Dear Cary,

I AM A faithful reader of your column and for many months wanted to send you this letter. My problem cannot be discussed with friends or family because part of the reason I am struggling with my life involves my children. Some might perceive anything I say against my children as a sign that I don't love them, which is not true.

Since I was 11 I have lived in a rich fantasy world that involved me being the princess at the party, the movie star at the premiere, a force that was admired and the object of desire, never picked last for the team. I was criticized a lot so it doesn't take Freud to figure out why I've immersed myself in fantasy, but the reality of my life couldn't be further from the dreams.

I also write and submit stories. I write about women who are married to men who are alcoholics; I write about women who have affairs out of a desperate need to escape the bleakness of their situation, but always get left because of their afore-mentioned desperation; I write about women who wish to be anyone but who they are at that moment. I write about me. I write about this because it is what I know and if it doesn't come out of me, I feel like I will flatten under its weight. I also harbor this fantasy that I will be published, but criticize and question myself, wondering who in their right mind would read anything I wrote.

I have been married for 18 years. We waited 12 years to have children and have three. My husband developed some negative habits after the children were born. Since then he's resolved them, but out of those habits came lack of income, my increased dissatisfaction with my life and the pressures of having to raise children who can be difficult amidst the turmoil. I know this isn't my children's fault, but I just want to flee. I've dug my fingers into my countertops until they turn purple in an attempt to hold myself back from walking out the door. But the reality is I cannot leave and he won't either. Every time someone asks me to do something, or I want to take some time for myself, I can't because I have no other childcare. I hear about old friends getting together and having fun, and missed opportunities to do the same. I feel trapped and crated.

I am 42 now and still long for the romance, adventure, excess and happiness that I have been fantasizing about for 32 years. And as I write this, I have tears streaming down my face because I feel like a petulant, whining child for even thinking these things. And yet I do think these things. I should be grateful and satisfied with what I have, but I always wonder what if. I can hear people yelling at me, telling me to grow up and stop acting like a spoiled brat, that life is what I make of it and it is all up to me—that things could be worse. I do know all of this. I know. And yet ... I wish for the tide to carry me out, but not drag me under.

*Waiting for This Moment to Be Free*

## Dear Waiting,

THESE VOICES YOU hear yelling at you, telling you to grow up and stop acting like a spoiled brat, these are not helpful voices. They are not what you need right now.

Perhaps you have lived with these voices a long time. They may be the voices of your parents and teachers. They sound like voices of trauma. Survivors of traumatic events sometimes seem to emerge with one burning truth, that life is a treacherous struggle for survival and that to entertain anything fanciful or sensual is to court disaster. Perhaps whoever raised you conveyed to you the belief that you must suppress all impulses toward the creative and fanciful, lest such impulses render you vulnerable and bring you to ruin in a hard and ruthless world. Perhaps this was conveyed in a spirit of love and protection. But it was a murderous thing to do to a person whose true survival depends on finding creative expression.

Not everyone is creative. But for those of us who are, it is a life-and-death struggle. We suppress these impulses at our grave peril. Eventually, one reaches a point of crisis such as you seem to have reached. It has become unbearable to suppress your creative side any longer. Your ability to ignore who you are is crumbling. Your authentic self is threatening to emerge, intimately bound up with these yearnings and visions you have been having since the age of 11.

> Your authentic self is threatening to emerge.

These voices threaten to murder that emergence, so you must counter them. You may feel that you are not allowed to turn and counter these voices, to disown them, to call them out and smash them, to bury them, to walk away from them. They may have protected you at certain times, buying you acceptance in a narrow, censorious society, keeping you from being branded insane, or an egomaniac, or a witch; perhaps it was seen as uppity and unrealistic to have any creative impulses; it may have seemed to you that in kowtowing to these voices you were keeping yourself within the bounds of consensus reality.

But it is time for you to embark on a journey full of amazement. The starting point is right there on the other side of these voices. So you need some tools to work with these voices.

Cognitive behavioral therapy is really great. It can help you.

I took a walk on the beach and it started to rain. I came home and messed around in the backyard, bringing in things that would get wet, watching a very long earthworm trek across the flagstones I had laid three years earlier. I was thinking that cognitive therapy would work wonders for you. I carried this thought inside with me and sat and thought, and found myself leafing through the April Sun magazine, reading an interview with shamanist Leslie Gray, and then I came back to your letter, even more convinced that these various longings and drives you are feeling are legitimate and must be honored.

Perhaps what you do is you start with cognitive therapy. But you move beyond it. You keep going. You keep going into richer realms. These realms, I am convinced by the tone and the strength in your letter, are right at your door—shrouded from view by these harsh, hectoring voices.

That intrusive, negative thought you have about being published—that no one in their right mind would read anything you wrote—also deserves to be countered and dismissed. It simply is meaningless. Obviously you can write. You will get published because you instinctively speak of true things, and these are things others also have experienced. So you will get published, not because you are special but because you are honest and you speak of your own experience, which mirrors the experience of many.

So find someone who practices cognitive therapy and see if you can do something about these self-murdering voices. It will probably happen fairly quickly, the dissolution of these idiotic, cruel voices. Emergence of the self that has been so long suppressed may take longer. That is OK. It is like the soul's emergence. It is like that earthworm whose patience I so admired as it inched across the vast patio of flagstones.

Then keep going. You have deep creative resources. This is obvious. Your vision and talent were awakened when you were 11 and you have been spending all this time tamping it down to get along and fit in; all these years you've been trying to be the person you were taught you were supposed to be, but this creative force, this life force, to its eternal credit, has not yet been killed or stifled. It can't be. You can't stop it. It will not go away because it is trying to save your life. It is a gift trying to be given to you. Receive it. Accept it. And then pass it on.

Citizens of the Dream:

# Overcoming Distractions, Beating Blocks and Getting it Done

# I get distracted by the Internet
# when I try to write

*Every time I start to do my assignment,*
*I find myself surfing the Web instead!*

**Dear Cary,**

I AM TAKING a creative nonfiction writing course, and I'm supposed to be working on a piece about what I ate for breakfast. The problem is, every time I sit down at the computer to work, I start compulsively reading the election coverage online, sometimes spending two hours or more on variations on the same five articles. I am ashamed of my lack of self-control in this area. It is really unusual for me, because in my normal life I am a very capable person. I am a stay-at-home mom of two boys, ages 8 and 6, with a great marriage. I keep a neat house, get the kids to school on time, and fix organic, gourmet meals. But in this one area, this writing class, I can't seem to do the task in front of me. I have always been a terrific student. I have a master's degree in anthropology from the University of Chicago, and until I got married, I always figured I would finish my Ph.D. and work in research or teach somewhere. Instead, I decided I wanted to be home with my kids and fix up our house. I learned to garden and bake pies, and basically dug my heels into domestic life. It suits me, as I am basically an introvert who likes to take care of people. I am happy here, but I see my kids growing up and not needing me as much, and rather than stifle them with overattentiveness, I decided to take some classes and get a hobby, as they say. The sewing class is going great; I've made a skirt and might work on curtains next week. But the writing class, the one I really care about, has me totally stumped. I can't seem to stop myself from clicking on the Google news page. Cary, is this self-sabotage, or simply escapism? What should I do? I've read that all writers need a lot of time to just sit and stare, but the Internet news is just wearing out my brain to the point where I can't work at all.

I'm afraid that I am not allowing myself to do the one thing I'd be really good at, maybe for fear of failure, or just because it seems too selfish. My mother worked at a high-powered job throughout my childhood, and my parents were divorced, so I have issues about being ignored as a kid. I swore that I would be the mom who made cookies and was always there when you needed her. The problem is, my kids don't seem to care one way or another, since they've never known any different. Cary, I feel sometimes like a doormat or a dishrag, like I am wasting all of my potential, and no matter how many Terence Conran house books I read or Julia Child cookbooks I memorize, I am still not getting what I need. I think I need this writing thing way more than I will admit to myself. So, how do I let myself just do it, without all of the distractions? On the other hand, am I just kidding myself with this fantasy that I might have great untapped potential? Maybe I should just accept the choices I've made and be happy planting tomatoes.

*Stumped*


Dear Stumped,

THERE ARE CERTAIN things you're just going to have to assume from the outset. Assume that your writing is important. Assume that you have the right to do it and that it's necessary and important. Assume that something has happened in your life such that you must attend to certain moral, aesthetic and philosophical needs, or that you have reached a certain passage, or phase, or that you have been blessed, contacted by aliens, touched by God, whatever works, however you want to put it. Something has happened. You have received a call. Assume whatever you need to assume in order to answer the call.

That is what I would suggest.

For that's what it is: It is a call. It might not be clear exactly what it is yet. But something is calling you and you have to answer the call. It might be frightening to answer—it might be asking you to face certain fears about your own competence and value. It may be asking you to take up a challenge. But I believe that whatever it is you are trying to accomplish, it is best to begin with your own motivation and your own desire, and work from that place, rather than concentrate on the phenomenon of distractions and try to eliminate them. You will find more energy in focusing

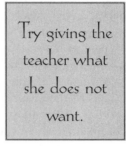

Try giving the teacher what she does not want.

on your objective than in focusing on defeating the distractions. Now, it's true, as a tactical matter, I often have to turn off my browser. I have to sit in silence. I have to find places and techniques. But the main thing is to find the deep emotional or spiritual hunger that fuels our creativity. Assume that this is important and you will find it easier to take the necessary steps. And as I said, you may be called to difficulty, to facing fears.

In facing your fears, I advise this: Guard against contemporary assumptions about cultural value, particularly our assumptions about what it means to be a writer. You are trained in anthropology. So look at our culture as an anthropologist would look at it. Notice the beliefs we express about writing and writers. Observe how we revere certain writers and vilify others. Notice that we seem to harbor some primitive belief in writing as a magical act; notice how we behave toward certain writers as though they were shamans or gods or priests; notice how as we do this we also devalue our own native abilities and thus become consumers rather than producers. Notice how we devalue our own desires to write, buying into such notions that only a select few are called to do this holy and sacred thing. See how undemocratic that is. Notice how much hogwash we are wading through. Keep all this in mind as you begin to write.

Also pay attention to what conditions allow you to write and what conditions hinder your writing. Where can you go to write? Can you park your car on a lakeside, sip a cappuccino and write? Can you take a trip and write? Can you sit in an attic room and write? How much time can you put aside to write? Can you use a timer? Have you tried free-writing? Is it possible that the nonfiction class you are taking does not offer productive methods? For instance, if you were simply told to go home and write about what you had for breakfast, it might be that such a thing does not work for you. I do not know if I could write about what I had for breakfast. I might feel compelled to think about it too much. Maybe if you started with, "Today for breakfast I had ..." then words might follow. You might end up writing, "Today for breakfast I had a fucking hard time of it." Or "Today for breakfast I had none of your fucking oatmeal." I don't know. You might find things arising that you did not expect. It is fun to see what words come. You might find anger and pain arising first. That is often the case. It may be that you do not want anger and pain to arise. That might be why you are not writing at all. If so, you may be helped by the support of a group. You might look around in your area and see if there are any groups that follow the writing process movement, or the Amherst Writers and Artists method.

Oh, here is something else: Part of writing seems to involve rebellion. One challenges the gods; one steals fire; one dares to create; one plays Prometheus. I note that you say you have been a good student. Good students do what they are told. Writers do what they are not told; they have to tell rather than be told, so a bit of rebellion is involved. Being a good student might be holding you back. Being a bad student might be better. It is fun to be a bad student for once. Be a bad student by disobeying the teacher. Try giving the teacher what she does not want. Try being bad. Try writing badly. Just put a mess of words down.

Let it go.

In other words, in order to overcome this habit of distractions, I recommend that you focus first on becoming who you are as a writer, and that you embark on a journey. I recommend that you enact a long-term plan, not just to start writing but to become a writer in the world. Join the worldwide community of writers.

Writing brings great rewards. It makes us happier. It entertains us. It allows us to know others in a unique way. It manifests what is hidden or unexpressed. This makes our lives deeper and more interesting. So, to paraphrase Baudelaire, get writing! Whether by wine, by poetry or by virtue, no matter! But get writing!

# The slush pile gave me writer's block!

*Everything was fine until I started reading unsolicited manuscripts.*

Dear Cary,

I'M A WRITER, though as of yet unpublished. I've written stuff I'm deeply ashamed of (a novel almost 10 years back that was horrid), and I've written stuff I genuinely like. A few years ago I sent a collection of flash fiction stories to a publisher, and although it didn't want to publish them, it replied with a personal letter in which it told me what worked and what didn't. A personal letter is a really big thing, so I was beyond thrilled. But then I made a huge mistake: I went to work in a small publishing firm, and during my time there became familiar with the slush pile. I should note that we don't use agents in my country, so people submit directly to the publisher. Hence the slush pile is one huge, ugly, throbbing pile of big dreams and bad writing. And these people have no idea how bad they are. Working at the publishing firm I started worrying about my own skills as a writer, and became unable to write anything for the next couple of years.

Thankfully, I've almost conquered the block now. This year I finally finished an old short story, and I've started working on a new novel. You know that old adage that in order to become a good writer you should write write write and read read read? Well, I really enjoy writing up impossible worlds, but I hate fantasy. The people in my stories often have something weird about them (wings, tails, the ability to get published), but they still live in regular cities. The story, setting and plot should be realistic, I think. Problem is, I don't really have any literary role models in this genre, so I fear my writing might end up as fantasy that no one will like. As I'm writing, I keep hearing my imaginary—but very literary—reader saying, "This stuff is totally unbelievable!" My big questions are: How do you believe in your own writing? I don't mean after it's finished, but while you're writing it? Is there a way to work with the imaginary reader instead of fighting with him/her? Thank you,

*The Slusher*

## Dear Slusher,

YOU WILL LEARN generosity toward your own work by becoming more generous to others. In the slush pile are the souls of people. They are perhaps badly dressed. But they are the souls of people, high and low. Honor them.

Yes, I know that much writing one will encounter in the slush pile will lack certain elements of organization and will employ devices that have not been reworked sufficiently to entertain us or do not show the marks of fine craftsmanship and years of study. But why should this bother us? All the author has done is render a work with a skill that we deem insufficient. What business do we have getting angry at such a person, or scoffing, or denouncing? Really, where does that come from? We say, Oh, this person is so intolerably presumptuous as to assume she can produce a work of fine fiction when ...! Oh, this person has no idea how hard it is, how many years it takes! How dare she!

Huh?

I think that anger comes from a fear of seeing ourselves in that work. We see ourselves as possibly inferior and we protect ourselves from that possibility by puffing up our scorn. It's the bluster of a frightened ego. It has nothing to do with our talent.

I should say this, too, right upfront: The operative question is not how do we believe in ourselves but how do we go forward? If you create this condition that you must believe in yourself to go forward, you might not go forward. You must find a way to go forward without that condition. You do not need to believe in yourself. You just need to find a way to move forward and embrace the activity you are engaged in. You think that believing in yourself will give you the strength to go forward? It may not work that way. It may be that you go forward simply by going forward.

On the other hand, there may be something historical at work. Read on:

OK, this is what happened to me, OK, and it had to do with my dad. So it's about 1993 or 1994, and I'm doing a series of magazine assignments for Details magazine about rock bands. And each time I do a piece, it gets accepted and I get paid but it doesn't run. And I'm maybe four or five years sober, and I'm working a shit job. Not the Chevron job—that was an OK job. This is a real shit job where they kind of hate me and stick me in a windowless room addressing envelopes by hand all day long. So I'm trying to do the freelancing and I'm having these heart palpitations and panic attacks when I have to call my editor. "My editor." What a phrase. The phrase even sort of freaks me out now. But anyway the one thing about my shit job is it has health insurance and an employee assistance program, so for the first time in my life I go see a therapist. (I'd tried before to get into therapy at the Jung Institute but they looked me over and decided I was a little rough on the edges.) So I go in for this quick session with a great guy who happens to be practicing some version of behavioral cognitive therapy. And at first I break down in tears, like I'm just a wreck, you know, and it all spills out, and I go, Wow, so this is therapy! Whee!

But long and short of it, we get to my problem that I can't pick up the telephone and call my editor. I mean I pace, I fret, I eat, I drink coffee, I read, I walk, I avoid. I can't call my editor. I'm

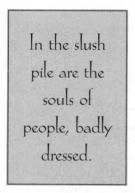

In the slush pile are the souls of people, badly dressed.

afraid. What am I afraid of? I dunno. So we talk. What it gets around to is my dad. My dad who gave me all these gifts, I think, this ability with words, this vocabulary, this sensibility. So I am thinking that my dad is not a frightening man, that he is, you know, my dad, and he's on my side. So we talk about these little voices in my head that say I can't write. And it turns out that these little voices that say I can't write sound a lot like my dad. Not that it's my dad talking, but that I've introjected my dad's disapproval of anyone who can't write, so that I'm afraid, actually, of being one of those people he would talk about who can't write. I had seen his harsh disapproval and I no way wanted to ever be one of those people so low in his estimation. Being his son, consciously I thought I was immune. I thought I, having standards and ability, was immune to the fear that I might not measure up. Big surprise. Because as a child, I didn't know if I had ability or not. I realized I was carrying around this childish fear of not measuring up to my dad's standards, even though consciously I thought everything was fine. I thought I was standing on the victory side, looking down on all those poor suckers who "can't write." And I also had been very mean. I had been an arrogant, mean person, puffed up and dismissive, curt and cutting. I thought that was how I was supposed to be.

But it turned out that I was actually living in fear of the judgment of others and—more important, since I had internalized this—actually living in fear of my own judgment! I thought that I was on the judging side of the judgment continuum, but I was actually, simultaneously, on the judgee side. So I think when we judge others harshly we run the risk of internalizing a fear that we ourselves will be judged the same way. Likewise, our harsh judging of others may at times be in reaction to this fear—it's a vicious circle. The way to stop it is to learn to love the slush pile. Learn to love the sheer production of language, I say! Learn to love the courage with which someone all alone out there in nowhereland gets it into his or her head to write a novel and sits down and does it. Honor that! Let us all honor one another!

We cannot judge harshly without also living in fear of being judged. And it is that creeping fear of being judged ourselves that can prevent us from writing fluidly and with ease and courage. So I say step out there and be really, really bad if you want. Who cares? Step out there and write the worst prose imaginable! So what? There's no law. Do it with gusto. Write the worst possible prose. Write poems that are so bad you can smell them. Do it. Look around. Have you been arrested? Have you been fired? Are you being held up to public ridicule? No. It's safe. It's safe to write whatever you want. And you never know. Some of the most awful stuff might be the best. You don't know. You can't judge your own work or control how others respond to it.

(Oh, and by the way, what actually helped me were the specific things I did in the course of the cognitive therapy, so you might just try that too!)

When we encounter prose we consider to be inferior and we ridicule it, we dig our own grave a little deeper every time. Because inside, the unconscious, I don't think it knows the difference. It's similar to this phenomenon in tennis where if you worry about hitting the ball into the net, you are more likely to hit it into the net. If you think, Don't hit it into the net, your dumb animal brain just seems to hear "in the net," and there it goes. Your animal brain is not registering the modifiers. It just hears "in the net." Because probably what you are doing there, although you are thinking verbally "not in the net," the image in your head is of a ball going into the net. And it is the image that your animal brain picks up on. So likewise, if you are looking at writing that you think is bad, it may not know that you are not a bad writer. It just sees/feels the emotional image of dejection and contempt. It just feels your contempt. If there's bad writing around, it doesn't know whose it is. So it gets all locked up in fear.

Therefore, given this understanding of the motivational structure of the brain: We celebrate writing, all writing! We celebrate it.

Let the taboos against bad writing fall, let the barriers come down, let the sharp-tongued English teachers take their seats and let us do what we do, and let those who would judge us go ahead and judge us—we don't care. We're going to do it anyway. Let them proclaim us as the dirty unskilled urchins of their nightmares. We are not living to please them.

I used to think I was on top, looking down on all that was awful. Now I feel that I am on the bottom of the sea looking up at everything that is marvelous!

You get where I'm coming from? So let us dance, all of us, together on the bottom of the sea.

# Why am I obsessed with celebrity gossip?

*Instead of writing poetry, I'm checking out IMDB.*

Dear Cary,

EVERY DAY I find myself logging on to a variety of Web sites—People.com, eonline.com, Salon's the Fix—to gobble up all forms of celebrity gossip. I spend hours on imdb figuring out which celebrities were born closest to my birthday (Billy Crudup, Robert Rodriguez) or discovering that both Debra Messing and Cate Blanchett named their sons Roman. After awards shows, I go to site after site to relive the dresses, the hairstyles, the snippets of gossip from the red carpet and the after parties.

It struck me that this was a problem again last night, when I read that Laura Dern and Ben Harper got married, then proceeded to Google them to death to find photos of them doing mundane things like walking with their baby down the street. They seem like cool people, but could I possibly care about the minutiae of their lives? And what about the hours I handed over to that endeavor?

I've always been fascinated with celebrities, but the fascination was for years limited to magazine browsing in line at the grocery store. Even then, I knew it was odd that I could tell you the names of Demi Moore's daughters (Rumer, Scout and Tallulah) without a pause. But lately, fueled by the whole-house wireless my news junkie partner installed, it seems I can't get enough.

I might not worry about this if I weren't worried about other elements of my life. My stunted creativity, for example. I'm a writer, but for years I haven't finished things that weren't on a specific work-related deadline. My own writing, though I sit down to it regularly, is shrinking. I've published a book of poems, been nominated for a Pushcart, taught creativity to both kids and adults. All this is past tense. I feel I'm getting less and less creative. It's harder to tap into the free-form spill that leads me into a poem, harder to wiggle into the voice that makes a story rise above the rote. I'm in one of those jobs that is too good to leave, too bad to stay. I drive to work fantasizing about quitting. I walk into my cubicle and I slump. On my days off and in the early morning, I work on my own pieces up to a point, and then I file them away. I read about why Renée Zellweger always wears Carolina Herrera.

Is this as simple as mere avoidance, distraction? Other things in my life are good. I'm in a happy partnership, have a relatively nourishing home life. I have good friends. The sun shines a lot where I live. My garden has fresh herbs.

I turn to you because you are so gifted at seeing beyond the obvious, at teasing out the nuanced reasons for the choices we make. I know that I can unplug the Internet, talk with my therapist, go cold turkey. I'm more interested in what lies beneath. Unlocking this seems the key to changing it. What is the metaphor here? What questions should I be asking? What might I be hungering for? I just read a story about a couple who searched for a year and a half for an apartment in Brooklyn with the right fireplace, and the moment they saw it, bought a studio with a mantel tiled with undulating dogwood carvings. They fell for a fireplace. There's something noble in that hunger. An update on Kirsten Dunst's hair extensions? Not so noble.

Can you help me see my way out of this, Cary? I've got

*Too Many Stars in My Eyes*


Dear Too Many Stars,

I SEE CELEBRITIES as gods and goddesses. A strong interest in their betrothals and betrayals, their binges and fasts, their tragedies, to me indicates an interest in the world of magical characters. It is at root a spiritual quest, closely allied with our thirst for literature. The reason we are so obsessed by celebrities today, I figure, is that there is nowhere else in our culture with such rich and readily accessible tales of such magical and entrancing variety.

Just, for instance, the lead item in the Fix today, as I'm writing, is this: "Gwyneth Paltrow has enlisted a rabbi from the Kabbalah Center to exorcise the ghosts from the five-bedroom London townhouse she shares with Coldplay frontman Chris Martin and their 19-month-old daughter, Apple. 'Gwyneth believes that the dark energy that has dogged her lately is due to something dark and unexplained in her home,' a source told Daily Mail. 'Her pregnancy is not as peaceful as her last one and she has also been upset by a stalker.'"

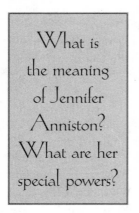

What is the meaning of Jennifer Anniston? What are her special powers?

Isn't that wild? (Note that she, as a vessel, holds our crazy beliefs so we don't have to.)

I would argue that gods and goddesses are only useful to us in our lives if they are not regarded consciously as gods and goddesses—only if they are regarded as real. I would suggest that we cannot possibly regard the gods and goddesses of another age and culture the way members of that culture themselves regarded their gods and goddesses. I figure that the ancient Greeks and Romans regarded their gods and goddesses much as we regard our film stars. The minute we become conscious of worship, the worship dies. It loses its magical power. We become self-conscious. So the obsession with celebrities is an act of primitive cultural innocence.

We have a pantheon of amazing figures; we are swimming in it; we are living in a magical world. It is natural for us to be transfixed by these characters because we are thirsty for magic. We are not satisfied with our earthly existence, nor should we be. We are humans and humans hunger for the divine. Our religions have failed us, our philosophies have failed us, our government has failed us, and our writers have ... well, nevermind. You get what I'm saying: Embrace celebrity worship! Do not be ashamed! It is a real hunger that you are feeding!

I would suggest that you build on your interest in celebrities in several ways. For one thing, try to understand your particular responses to particular celebrities in terms of your own interests and struggles. What do your likes and dislikes of various celebrities say about you as a person, your aspirations, your secret hopes, your values? Expand on this. Perhaps you could keep a journal or a scrapbook. Perhaps you could embark on something akin to fan fiction, using the gods and goddesses of our media world as characters in tales of your own creation. Or perhaps, using readily available video software, you could create movies of your own with digital images of stars found on the Internet. If you are a writer and feel your interest is taking you away from writing, I would suggest bringing your writing to bear on your interest.

As for me, I also have a private pantheon of characters about whom I feel deeply, but they are boring and embarrassing. For instance, my secret sorrow lately has been the disappearance of Aaron Brown from CNN. I find his being supplanted by the crass young "360" man quite disappointing; while I found him at first, as I said in an e-mail to a colleague back when Brown started, a little unctuous. But after a time I came to enjoy Brown's avuncular style. Primarily what I enjoyed was his judgment—the professional sifting and sorting of stories. This was an appreciation mostly of craft, of how someone works; but then I am a fairly work-centered person. I also liked the fact that Aaron Brown was not trying to make me feel anything (this is very telling about me). I resent the attempts of newspeople to make me feel. I do not want to be made to feel—especially by newspeople. I feel plenty already. I am not deficient in feeling. I am deficient in understanding. I grit my teeth every time Anderson Cooper comes on the screen. I resent him. I wish he would go away. I wish him a bad fate of some sort, I'm not sure what—perhaps that he would fall into the mud. If I were a child playing with little figures of newspeople, I think I would make Anderson Cooper fall in the mud and have to crawl around in it.

That probably says a lot about my primitive drives and fears, perhaps more than I would like to know.

What do I like on television? I like History Channel World War II stuff with bombs and fighter planes. I like stuff like "What if the moon disappeared?" Because at heart, I'm a little comic-book science boy, fascinated by strange tales of the earth! (This is a clue to my mythic life.) Frankly, all those celebrities remind me of the pain of being an outsider in high school. I feel more comfortable identifying with grim scientists.

So it's interesting for me to think about this in relation to my own life. And it's interesting to note, as I consider it, how strongly I feel about these things! Aaron Brown's departure was a genuine personal loss, about which I might have written an essay if I did not fear seeming foolish. Or, more precisely, if I did not fear parading my personal feelings without any kind of argument to back them up. It was just a personal thing.

Point being, it's interesting and instructive to ask ourselves what we like about celebrities. It tells us more about ourselves than perhaps we would like to know. So if I were you, rather than fighting your interest in celebrity lives, I would try to build on it, take it to a deeper level, make an art of it. Especially since you are a writer: Your subject is right in front of you. What is the meaning of Jennifer Aniston and Brad Pitt? What are her special powers? What does she represent? I do not know, but you probably do.

# I'm rewriting the same paragraph over and over and over!

*I'm stuck creatively and don't know where to turn.*

**Dear Cary,**

I'M BLOCKED. CREATIVELY, spiritually, emotionally—you name it. I'm a 28-year-old writer who can't seem to get anything onto the page without second-guessing and editing the entire time. I write the first sentence over and over, eventually giving up on the idea entirely—only to see it appear in another publication later. This happens constantly.

(It took me an hour to write that first paragraph. If this were a piece, and not a messy letter, it would've taken me four.)

But this writing block, really, is just one facet in a complex problem. It's merely a symptom, not the cause, of my distress.

A little back story: I've spent a lot of time in various creative pursuits. Moved to NYC for film school, ditched it to come home and form a band, which ended up making several records and touring for years. I had lots of friends and all these fantastic experiences. I felt connected, truly.

When the band ended (along with a really awful five-year relationship), I took to freelance writing. I also took to drinking and generally being a debaucherous mess, but it felt like such an incredibly important time—I had even more friends (a few of whom are still my bestest) and even more experiences, and it was just so much fun, I can hardly stand to think about it.

But then all the fun got tedious. I met a similarly debaucherous boy (now my husband) and together, we kicked most of our bad habits. Stopped going out as much, laid off the drugs and drinking, and just enjoyed being relatively functional, in-love 20-somethings.

Several months later, after a complete financial breakdown, I bit the bullet and got a real job at a real corporation willing to pay me real money. At first, it was novel and hilarious, just another silly experience, but two years later ... here I am. Not that it's awful; not by any stretch. It is a writing job, after all, and it's in a field I've come to adore. I absolutely love my co-workers, two of whom have become great friends, and my husband and I actually have money; a strange thing for two kids who cut their teeth on the '90s riot grrrl/hardcore scene and have spent their lives in either touring vans or punk houses.

But now, suddenly, I feel stuck. Blocked. I moonlight for a totally amazing publication and my husband and I have just started a two-person music project, but it's a struggle for me to actually finish anything. I write and write and write, and then give up. I never leave the house, even though I want to, and I always feel like I'm not having any fun when my husband does manage to drag me out. I go to bed really, really early. And I'm absolutely disconnected from everyone in this city; the scene/community/whatever that used to feel like home to me is now just this strange, strange place that I have no hope of navigating. The few people that I do know (holdovers from years past) are all doing these amazing things; opening shops, running really great club nights, starting businesses. Some are still touring and recording. I just go to work and come home. My life has become totally about my job and not the work I really want to be doing, the things I ideate and never execute. Granted, my job carries a tiny bit of prestige, but I don't ever see it that way. I just feel old, stodgy and upwardly mobile.

Thing is, I know what I need to do. I know I need to go out and experience things again, to not stare at these same four walls day after day. I know I need to write for the sake of writing and not be concerned about the fate of whatever I finish. I know I need to stay in touch with old friends and try to make new ones, to travel when I can, to invite people over and write letters and live. I know this. But when I make a list of all the things I need to do, I feel so overwhelmed that I end up curling up in a ball and falling asleep. I'm not lazy, I'm not unmotivated, I'm just ... stuck.

Cary, how do get past this life block and experience things again? How do I stop being so intimidated and overwhelmed by everything not work-related? Because though I love my job, it's just a job. It's what I do to make the money to do other things, yet it's all I think, feel and breath. I need more ... but how do I get it?

*Quicksand*

Dear Quicksand,

I HAVE JUST taken some Percocet. Because I have chosen to continue writing the column as I recover from minor but painful surgery, it has been necessary to write while under the influence of painkillers and opiates. This presents a challenge for someone with a history of drug abuse.

But my hope is that it also presents possibilities. And so, for the third day, I write in a new way. The rule I have made for myself is that I cannot go back and fix, or rearrange, or rewrite what I have done. I realized, on the first day of this experiment, when I absolutely lacked the mental concentration to do that kind of rearranging, that I would have to give it up. Thus I was forced to write this new way.

I recommend this to you. Even now, as I try to form the thoughts, or arguments, that I feel are persuasive in this regard, they remain elusive. What I am accustomed to doing I cannot do. This disability is forcing me to simply keep writing and moving forward.

Of course I fear that I will not be brilliant enough. This fear will have to wait. I cannot hide from it.

Your plight raises many questions for me.

The previous seems to me to be veering close to incoherence. So I will attempt to ground this. I have just paused to have breakfast with my wife and have conversations about my past. Now I am back, with a cup of coffee, rereading your letter. I will now attempt to talk about two things. One is the way that taking a corporate job can affect you more deeply than you at first realize. The other is how a few simple grounding activities may help you to begin moving forward again.

First, from my own experience: Like you, I did many creative things early in life and then tried to settle down. I, too, took a corporate job for a few years. What I would caution you about, from my own experience, is the danger of renouncing your former belief in the primacy of creative experience. In joining the corporate economy, you face a genuine choice.

In spite of what you believe is possible—that it is possible to "have your day job and keep your integrity"—my experience has been that the concrete, day-to-day forces, sociological and economic, that hold corporations together and make them function, will and must work on you; they will force you to choose. You cannot maintain two completely separate lives. What you are experiencing now, it seems to me, is the pain—the terror, perhaps—of realizing that your occupation must take all of you. I believe that this would take many paragraphs to argue in detail, and as I have said, since I am somewhat impaired, I cannot make that argument in full. Yet this is my strong intuitive sense: that you will continue to be in turmoil as long as you try to succeed in your corporate job and also live a full and inspired creative life outside it.

So, because of this untenable situation, it might be said that your blockage is a kind of symbolic resistance. It is both a symbolic resistance and it is symptomatic. In other words, not only are you resisting being consumed by the corporation, but you are also already feeling the debilitating effects of being in the corporation. Already, you cannot function as an artist the way you formerly did. Yet you continue to try. Your blockage is telling you: You can't do this! Yet you have so far avoided accepting the situation.

So you keep trying to do the impossible. You overestimate your capacity and underestimate the power of the corporate life to sap you of that capacity. Thus you are stuck. Or, more pre-cisely, you feel stuck. You are not actually stuck, any more than a man who keeps trying to climb up the sheer side of a building is stuck. He persists in trying the impossible. But he has a choice. He can recognize that what he is doing is impossible. His options are to either find something he can climb, or give up climbing.

So that is my opinion about how your corporate work is affecting you. My other comment, as I promised, is about how you may regain your ability to move forward creatively. This interests me a great deal right now because what you describe in your first paragraph is what I have fallen prey to repeatedly. Now that I simply cannot hold several thoughts in my head at once, now that I am forced to move in a strictly linear way, I feel a break-through is at hand. I would like to say a couple of things about it, one specu-lative and the other quite a concrete suggestion. My speculation is that one motive for being stuck, spinning our wheels and the like, is that we are trying to stop time. Perhaps we fear what we are proceeding toward. In the case of writing and rewriting a paragraph 20 times or 50 times, we may fear the plainness and simplicity of what is in our minds; we may fear that unless we unleash a dazzling fusillade of verbal inventive-ness, the reader will turn away in boredom and disgust. So we keep tinkering, trying to perfect the bomb.

> We fear the plainness and simplicity of what is in our minds.

And behind this need to have such an effect, we might say, is the need for power—power over the reader rather than with the reader. We are seeking a position of power and dominance; to simply speak in even, measured tones of our own experience will not give us that power and dominance; we have to "slay" the audience. We have to prove ourselves worthy. And this need to show ourselves worthy arises out of an unfortunate belief that we are in some sense not worthy—otherwise, why would we be trying so hard to prove it?

My other contention, that we are symbolically trying to stop time, is harder to convey. Perhaps I am not even correct in this. But I picture an animal furiously pedaling to nowhere. Language is a linear medium; it does not occur as a mosaic; it cannot be taken in all at once; it must unfold. It must occur in time. So by trying to perfect a paragraph, to make it like a bomb that explodes with wisdom, is to oppose the nature of narrative itself. It may be what imagist poets were trying to do, to induce ephemeral epiphany. So it is a very specialized use of language. Enough about that. It is a minor point I have already spent too much time on.

So, as to what concrete things you might do to get out of this hellish block: I would suggest what I am doing right now. Not that you have to take Percocet (I am acutely aware of the dangers of prescription drug addiction, and do not recommend any sort of experimentation in this regard). But begin unspooling, as I am unspooling. Begin simply writing forward, word by word.

One way is to stop writing on a computer. As we read texts from hundreds of years ago and think about how these texts were created, we must envision how writers worked without being able to move blocks of text around. They started at one end and continued toward the other end. Try this. It entails some fear. I may not appear as brilliant to you as I would like to appear. But I am not hiding. I am doing it one word at a time. There is no hidden process by which I am arranging what you read. I am here with you, in the moment, unspooling this.

Try this. Relax your shoulders. Write in a notebook. Begin with a first sentence. Write as you follow your thoughts. Note your thoughts and write them. Try to envision what you have to say, and imagine that you have the world's most engaged and patient, interested friend and reader on the other end, appreciating your words as they unspool, nodding thoughtfully at what you write. Imagine a person who wants to hear the whole story, told with some structure and coherence. Keep in mind that one of the primary things we love about words and about music is that they continue, that they simply continue, that we can slip into the stream of another's tale or song and for that time we are exempted from woe, we are in another's arms, we are wrapped in a story. Write from the beginning, as if to a friend, and trust that the friend keeps asking you, "Go on, please, what happened next?"

I have probably said enough. Looking over this, though, I have at least one more thought to share, and that is that you may be experiencing symptoms that require professional attention. It would not hurt, in fact, to at least discuss some of this with a psychological professional. Certain things you mention—your sleeping a lot, your not leaving the house—may be just ways that you are trying to cope with too much overwhelm, or they may be symptoms of some clinical problem. So please do not consider me an authority on any kind of mental disorder. I am not. I am not trained for that. I have availed myself of much professional help when I felt I might need it. So please keep that in mind.

Thus ends Day 3 of writing without a net. I do not mean to denigrate the practice of rewriting many times. I am sure that if you compare this text to other texts in which I have unleashed volleys of unrestrained ranting and have explored certain images that occur, and tried to decode them, and tried one beginning after another until I found the one most arresting, and cut out transitional sentences and qualifying modifiers, and experimented with rhythm and sound and combinations of different rhetorical devices, I am sure you will see that this is not a virtuosic performance. But it is a true performance. It is just me talking to you, not trying to dazzle you or floor you. There is something to be said for that. There is something to be said not only for its value as a product, but also for the process. When we are stuck revising and revising, we can forget that it's sometimes OK to just write straightforward prose.

This raises one last interesting question: Once the surgical incisions have healed and I am no longer in need of painkillers, will I continue to write in this fashion? What I hope to learn is that some revision is fine, but enough is enough. I hope also to learn to look far enough ahead, as I work, so that the work has a natural movement toward conclusion. But enough about me. In conclusion, I suggest you do two things. One, recognize and admit to yourself that there's no way you can succeed in corporate life and also continue your creative life with the same vibrancy and commitment you previously had. And two, to overcome this block, try denying yourself permission to revise. Just put the pen to paper and start moving forward. Keep going. Envision your ideal reader. Write to that person. Just keep going. Keep your eyes on the road far ahead; keep moving toward the next town.

# Dear Sir, I write today to say that I cannot write

*The perceived inability to write leads to an obvious contradiction—and an existential crisis.*

**Dear Cary,**

I'M NOT LOOKING for a cure so much as an assessment, I guess. Here's the "problem": I used to love to write. I wrote for my own enjoyment, all the time, starting pretty much from the moment I'd gotten the hang of the alphabet. Mostly I considered this separate from school interests and career ambitions, although more recently I'd been contemplating a career that would involve writing.

But I had a few bad "life experiences" that left me more cynical about other people and about my own instincts. And then I stopped writing. This seemed fine for a little while: I had more pressing concerns, and I figured I needed some time to recover anyway. The thing is, I've had time to catch my breath; my life is on track now, after it took a sharp left a ways back, and yet I can't start writing again.

I don't want to be a writer anymore, and that's cool, I don't see it as a problem. What worries me is that I can't write for the hell of it, just to myself. A couple of people connected with those disillusioning experiences were "writers"—aspiring, not professional, writers, and not very good ones, but it was my source of introduction and main point of connection with each of them. I've known plenty of people who were decent human beings and decent writers, yet now I find myself associating writing with the sleazy narcissism of those few bad apples. Then again, maybe it's not really about them so much as the fact that I haven't written since that series of unpleasant experiences; maybe the bigger problem is that I lived so much of my life alongside the parallel narrative in my notebooks, and I don't know how to resume that narrative now that there's been a break in it.

It may be for the best. I've changed from the person I was before, and I'm heading off on a different path now—maybe this is just one more old habit I ought to leave in the past. But I also wonder if I'll need it anyway, so as not to grow blinkered or unreflective. I'm not into therapy, and I'm more circumspect than I used to be about opening up to other people, so I worry a little about how I'll process the world without writing. Still, every time I sit down to write just for myself, I feel either total blankness or an overwhelming disgust that makes me want to get rid of everything I've ever written (which I've already done anyway).

Should I embrace the extra free time and channel it into more productive habits? Should I try to replace writing with something else? (Though I should add, I make a pretty lousy musician and I can't afford a lot of fancy art supplies.) Perhaps I'm just too accustomed to navel-gazing, and doing less of it would actually be more healthy. What do you make of this?

*Not a Writer*


Dear Not a Writer,

I WONDER HOW you managed to write this letter.

I don't mean to be facile. I mean, really, how did you manage it? You found yourself with a problem. You found yourself in pain. You had a reason to write. You knew how to write. So you wrote.

Writing is a life-and-death act of consciousness. It must be or we cannot continue. It brings us face-to-face with who we are. Hence the disgust and nausea. Hence the need for compassion.

Hence the need for understanding. Hence the need for honesty. Say we write something and as a result we are hurt. We seek to avoid hurt. So we stop writing in order to avoid the hurt. But writing is also a way to heal the hurt. So when we stop writing we fail to heal. So the wound festers. It gets worse and worse.

That is the cycle of destruction. Where we once castigated ourselves for writing poorly, now we castigate ourselves for not writing at all. It gets worse and worse and worse until we put the shotgun in our mouth. That is one cycle— of fear and paralysis and eventual suicide.

> I am sitting next to you in the lifeboat as we row, complaining that we cannot row.

But here is the other cycle: We write to find out who we are. We look at what we have written and we are stunned. We experience perhaps a moment of revulsion, of disgust: This is who I am!? Somebody shoot me! But then we think, what's wrong with that?

And we come to the fork in the road: Do we hide, then? Do we hide the identity that has emerged? That is the route of anorexia. We starve ourselves of being in order to hide what we are. OK, you could do that. But you're killing yourself. Why are you killing yourself? Because you don't deserve to exist? Because you don't deserve to be who you are in front of others? Do others have so much power over you? Why? Who gave them such power? The king? Who is the king? Is there a king? Is there a judge? Then we must be revolutionary and destroy the kings and the judges so we can be who we are without fear.

Why not be revolutionary and claim the right to exist as we are— to exist as we have revealed ourselves to be, in all our flawed majesty and brilliant failure? Why not step forward and say yes, this is who I am, fuck 'em if they can't take a joke. After all, we must remember that we are not entirely responsible for who we are. We did not create ourselves. We'd like to be better, maybe, but this is who we are. Must we apologize? To whom? To what king? To what judge?

Why not celebrate ourselves instead? For soon we will be gone! Now at least we exist. Our "mere" existence, as far as I can tell, is some kind of miracle.

So writing, even bad writing, becomes an act of revolutionary assertion: I am who I am. Deal with it.

My suggestion to you, my friend, is to forget all about using writing to get over. And forget about becoming a so-called good writer. Forget judgment and failure. Forget using writing for anything but revelation, however boring, however ugly, however mundane, however true.

# I'm making progress in my art but feel like it's all a dead end

*I've had some successes and some design internships, but I think I should move to Australia.*

Oh Cary,

I HOPE YOU can help me! I am 27 and live in a house, rent-free, that my parents own. A few years ago I was living in a different city while I was waiting tables and trying to make my art and design dreams come true on the side. I moved here with my younger sister so she could attend law school, with the intention of making a life/career for myself here. Needless to say, that has not happened. I have had a lot of small professional successes but nothing that I could ever live off of. At one point I found myself working in an accounting department for over a year, at which point I woke up and realized that I had to forge a creative career for myself or I would die by throwing myself in front of a dolly loaded with file boxes. So, over six months and two dead-end design internships later, I am still unemployable and don't seem able to employ myself.

Things are getting dire: I have no job and no income besides my piddling freelance gigs, and Mommy and Daddy are begging me to tell them what they can do to help me. My mother insists that I go back to school. I am starting to warm up to the idea by seeing friends my age going back to school. And by realizing that clearly my job skills aren't cutting the mustard, and even if I did find an employer that appreciated my talents, I would never be able to leave—because it would probably be the only one that ever wanted me! And I do not want that. I want options. Millions upon millions of options. So a master's degree it must be.

But (and here we come to the problem) the place I most want to go is in Australia, where I have dual citizenship and can work and go to school free. My mother is Australian and came here when she was young, intending to go back, and she never did, which of course caused all sorts of strife and heartache for her and her family. My mother has been vehement about neither my sister nor I ever going abroad because she is simply afraid we will not come back. A reasonable fear, I guess. But stifling! It's possible I have no genuine interest in living abroad, but because the idea has always been forbidden I want it very much. So this has been an ongoing argument in my family—me threatening to go or just showing an interest in going out of the country, and my parents and sister telling me all the reasons why I shouldn't and breaking me down until I just want to be left alone. And so I give up the idea. We're a close-knit bunch.

But the big problem is that I have a dog. I love this dog; she is like an extension of my personality. She follows me everywhere. I have never been away from her for more than 10 days. If I want to actually go abroad I would have to decide whether to take her with me (and in Australia there is a mandatory quarantine, and it's a looooong plane ride), which, honestly, does not sound like a good time for her or for me, or to leave her with my parents. My parents love her as much as I do and are always jokingly but kind of seriously asking me to let her come live with them. And then in the next breath they criticize me for being willing to leave the country and abandon her.

The whole point of me going abroad, and fulfilling a lifelong dream, is to declare my independence from my parents. Every plan I have for this move—starting school halfway across the world—involves saving money first. It takes a lot of $$ to get to Australia and back these days. So I want to be prepared. And what's the best way to save money? Living with your parents. And there's the rub. How can I possibly be asserting my independence from them while also asking them to house me while

I save money waiting tables, and take care of my dog and my boxes of stuff while I am away? I feel that my only two options are to forge on ahead with this plan, ignore my self-loathing for abandoning my beloved pet—or to stay here for an additional two years, go to a similar program here (which seems subpar but costs the same), and continue to live on the cheap in the House That My Immaturity Bought. I don't really want to do the second one. Mostly because mentally I have already checked out of living here, in this city, and especially in this house.

So ... I am ready for those words of wisdom.

*Anonymous*

Dear Anonymous,

YOU ARE ENGAGED in a project and you are making progress. But you speak of your project as if it were a failure. It is not a failure. It is a beginning.

What is this project? It is the building of a creative career.

You say, "I have had a lot of small professional successes." You say you have had two internships. But you say the internships were "dead ends," and the small professional successes were "nothing that I could ever live off of." Perhaps you thought, in each instance, that the internship or the small professional success would lead to a full-time design job. If so, your expectations were not realistic. What happened is this: You completed your professional assignments. You completed your internships. They were not failures. They were successes. They were completed. You finished them.

Now you move on to new assignments. Eventually, over time, your assignments grow in scope and become more numerous. You become more skilled and better known. You acquire business skills along with your artistic and creative skills. You build a creative career. You do it step by step.

You are in a great and enviable position. You have time. You have support. You have family. You are loved and cared for. You are at the beginning of your creative career.

And yet you are poised to upend it all by moving to Australia.

I understand that you are impatient and dissatisfied with your life. But going to Australia would be a symbolic solution to an actual problem.

You don't need to go to Australia. What you need to do is deal emotionally and creatively with your life right here and now. I suspect that aside from the very good school that is in Australia, the romance with Australia is related to your struggle with your mother. Her story has a great pull on your psyche.

> It is not a failure. It is a beginning.

This is the mistake we creative people make over and over again. Because creatively or spiritually we are in the forest, we think suddenly it is time to live in the forest. So we sell the house. We translate our inner lives into practical action that makes no sense. We wake up in the forest but we have left our paints behind.

We need to be working this stuff out in the medium that has chosen us, be it paint or sound or words. We get into trouble when we are not working these things out in our art. Our lives get out of control because we mistake the symbolic for the actual. And we need to work hard, exhaustively, on this symbolic material, or it will continue to present itself as actual; we will be hallucinating.

The truth is, we have to live in the practical world just like everybody else. We do our work, we make a modest income, we get up day after day and face a new and strange world, and every day we get a little better at it.

I think what you need is a plan. Your plan is concrete and has a time limit. Say it is a one-year plan, with a goal of doubling your income from creative work over that time, and developing the infrastructure that will allow you to grow and prosper in the design business. That means establishing ways of getting more work: using contacts, advertising, etc. Just set yourself a one-year goal.

And then you begin your lifelong practice. Year by year, maybe you make more, maybe less. But every year you do a little better. If you need more education you can go back to school in your area.

We build slowly on our accomplishments and we stand in line with everyone else and we work honestly and bravely and sometimes exhaustively for little gain. We keep at it day after day because we know that even if we are not getting what we think we should get for what we are doing, we are doing what we are meant to be doing. We build our business as we go.

You are in a great situation now. You are able to start something that is wholly yours, exactly what you want to do, and make it grow. You do not have to make a great living yet. You can take two or three years to get it where it will support you. Your parents are willing to help you. Your start-up costs are low. Your month-to-month costs are low. You are in an ideal situation.

You want a feeling of independence and self-sufficiency. The way to get a feeling of independence and self-sufficiency is by attaining those things concretely. You become self-sufficient and independent by taking certain actions. The feeling will come from the proof, from the tangible. You do not have to go to Australia to achieve that. You can be independent in the house you are living in that is owned by your parents.

In two or three years after you have this thing up and running, then you can go to Australia. You can take your mother with you. I'll bet it would mean a lot to her.

# I'm an interesting, talented artist but I can't take the rejection!

*I know it's part of the game, but it's beginning to defeat me.*

Dear Cary,

I'M AN ARTIST—IT'S the thing I've had since childhood, the thing I took for granted.

So I took it for granted and followed other paths—writing fiction and filmmaking.

I went to grad school, I published some books and many articles (nonfiction). I wrote (and sold) some screenplays. I directed some films and produced some TV shows.

So I'm sorta successful, but I still feel that "artist" is my life's calling. It's what I'm best at and what I love. And yes, I go through all the crap too—the stress, the inaction, the procrastination and so on, but I really feel it's what I was born to do. People like it—smart people, the people I'd hoped would like it, and they like it for the right reasons. I sell enough out of my studio to counter my expenses (not huge but significant nonetheless). I've been selected for juried shows by curators of major museums and been waitlisted on grants and residencies that are awarded to emerging contemporary artists—exactly where I'd hope my artwork would fall within the giant spectrum of the art world.

But it has yet to pay off with true success: representation by a gallery, which is the equivalent of getting an agent and all that that would hopefully bring.

In the meantime I have to work as a producer (lucrative, challenging, creative but I sublimate my own interests to be "mainstream" enough to be functional in this world) and then, while I'm working on freelance producing jobs, I have to get the rejection letters from things I've applied to. I realize I can't get accepted to everything I apply to, but each time I get rejected, it takes me down a notch, if only for that day. And then I recover (or forget) and go back to making art, and I've realized that this whole creation/rejection dichotomy actually creates the sort of manic-depressive (or bipolar) worldview that artists are known for: You get all excited about some idea and work in a creative frenzy and then you get a rejection notice and feel like "What the fuck am I doing anyways?"

My problem right now is that I don't get the "manic" highs of creation because I'm doing a freelance producing job which is very, very time-consuming (and creativity-consuming), so I can't make my own art at the moment and yet I am getting the "depressive" rejection letters that send me into a downward spiral for which there is no "manic" corrective. And I start to think, maybe "producer" is all I get to be; after all, I worked hard to get to be that too!

I don't think that I should give up on the artwork (I don't think I can, literally. I think I'd be miserable. It's pretty much my higher purpose in life). But how do I deal with the rejection during these periods where I can't make up for it with creative zeal? Because it's so fucking easy to get a rejection notice in the middle of the day at work on the cheesy TV show and think, "Who the fuck am I to think I am an artist?"

S.

## Dear S,

I AM A very critical person. If you are doing something and I am watching, I will have a different idea how you should do it, and I will take you apart and not even realize I am doing it until

I have ruined your experience. Then I will apologize. I will say I was just trying to help. Then I will go deeper and admit I am a destructively critical person. So I have this. I am critical of you and I am also critical of me.

Now, I also have high expectations. I have experienced litera-ture that opened the skies for me, that made the earth tremble, that proved the existence of a world right alongside ours, so far superior to ours that one might as well commit suicide. I have had these experiences with literature. So I expect a lot when I read. I have high expectations.

But that means I have high expectations for myself as well when I write. Every time I write I think I am required to make the skies open. I think I have to make the earth tremble. I think I have to reveal the existence of a dazzling universe quietly super-seding our own, right next to us in another dimension.

That is of course impossible—as well as being destructive. Realistically speaking, maybe once in my life I'll write something pretty good. Maybe twice.

So I have unrealistic expectations of myself and of other people.

So naturally I fail every day. And so does everyone else in my eyes. That is not a very comfortable world to live in, where I am failing every day, and everyone around me is failing every day too.

It became clear to me a while ago that if I went on writing in this kind of hell I would not last. If you have a voice in your head that is telling you every day that you suck and you can't write, because the heavens are not splitting open and the earth is not trembling, you're not going to last long. You're going to find yourself depressed. You're going to be paralyzed, unable to send out manuscripts.

You need constant encouragement and reinforcement in order to keep going. It's not even about feeling good so much. It's just about keeping going.

I began to think about athletes. I thought, what do athletes do? Are they rejected every time they perform? A batter gets a hit maybe every four or five at bats. So that's pretty tough.

How would an athlete deal with all that rejection?

In sports there is rejection and pain. But there is also joy and encouragement. There are coaches. There are teammates.

Those of us who work alone trying to make the heavens open up and the earth tremble, we need regular encouragement. We need coaches to say, Hey, good game. We need hand slaps and high-fives. Without support we will stop sending out our work. (Most of us, anyway. There are some who are like diamonds inside, brilliant and hard and unreachable. But most of us, we're sensitive.)

So, having never been, by temperament or upbringing or cultural leaning, a workshop person, and having had only the worst experiences in graduate school workshops, I nevertheless began looking for some organic forms of support. The only thing I knew in terms of groups was support groups for addiction and alcohol. I thought something along that line might work, but I had no idea what. I just knew that the unconscious needs to be cradled and encouraged.

> How would an athlete deal with all that rejection?

So browsing in Borders last fall before a long plane ride, I saw that book *Writing Alone and With Others*. I liked the title. It was sufficiently descriptive and exact. It did not promise me that I could write a novel in 30 days. It did not address problems of self-esteem that I did not have. It spoke to me.

So I read it and became convinced that the workshop method it outlines could help me and others improve our relationships with our own creative selves and with each other as creative people. So last week I completed a weeklong workshop with the author of that book, Pat Schneider, and was reinforced in my belief that this is the way to go.

We critical types are hard on ourselves. I have been very hard on others but I have believed it was OK because I was also very hard on myself. Others have been hard on me as well, and I have sort of invited that. I have said, That's OK, give it to me straight, I can take it. Actually, I couldn't take it. But I would say I could. I believed in the interest of telling it like it is that everybody had to be hard on everybody else and on themselves. That would ensure that we were all aesthetically honest and pure.

Well, so now I am thinking, what good does that do if we become so embittered and afraid of rejection that we can't continue our work? I think what we need is more acceptance and more love. But how do I become more accepting of myself? Well, if being hard on others and being hard on myself are so closely linked, perhaps being accepting of others and accepting of myself are also linked. So what if I were start being easier on others, and then eventually perhaps easier on myself? That is what happened in this workshop. We sat around and talked only about what we liked and what we remembered. We didn't tear each other up. Dangerous things were allowed to be said, and were said. They were said well. It was an atmosphere in which the dangerous and difficult things could be said. I was pretty amazed. It produced good work, to my mind, because the good work is the difficult work. It is the work that says things on the edge of acceptable.

So to you, fellow sufferer, I would say that you must build into your life some support systems. You may say that you know you are good. That is fine. I know I am good too. Still, I need to hear it every day. You may know that you are loved as well. You still need to hear it every day. You need to be told. And you need to tell others.

Another thought that prevented me from participating in workshops was this: Well, I'm a professional. I'm different. I'm better.

What I found was that as a professional I had certain things I could contribute. But it did not make me any better than anyone else. Rather, I stood in surprised awe. I said, What, you are not publishing? My God! It was astonishing.

So now in spite of my long-cultivated anti-workshop bias and my pride and my ego and my defensiveness and my well-suppressed desire to crush all other artists, in spite of my debilitating expectation that every word ought to split the sky or make the earth tremble or hint at the existence of a fantastic other world, in spite of my fear and my anger and my feeling of hopelessness and despair, I believe in the workshop.

It's what you have to do. Something inside you needs it.

There is much more to be said about this, but I think that is enough for now. There are cultural and political implications. There are spiritual implications. But that is enough for now. It's about the workshop. It's about finding structured support. It's what you have to do.

By the way, one practical way to avoid the crushing futility of never-ending rejection is to have a friend send out your work for you. This little tip came to me from Pat Schneider. The trick is to work with a friend. You send out your friend's work, and your friend sends out yours. Your friend gets the rejections but doesn't tell you. You don't need to know. When something encouraging happens, then your friend gives you the news.

# Now that I've got my master's in writing ... I'm not writing!

*I do well with things I know I'm great at,*
*but I'm not sure I'm great at writing.*

**Dear Cary,**

I'M A REASONABLY happy, reasonably successful 28-year-old woman. Since moving to Chicago from Ann Arbor, Mich., five years ago, I've done fairly well as a personal trainer at an upscale health club. I've got a great apartment, good friends and a wonderful boyfriend with whom I live. This past June, I earned my master's in writing, finally attaining the knowledge and experience I thought I might need to change careers and pursue writing full time. Though much of my background is in fitness, my plan has long been to stick with training only until I could secure a writing job or switch to training part time and writing freelance. My friends, my family and even my professors have been enormously supportive of this plan. Now, nine months later, the question I've come to dread is, "How's the writing going?" The honest answer, which I always—albeit begrudgingly—supply, is that it's not. Aside from a deliriously short-lived venture into fitness blogging, I've stalled in my attempts to produce anything worthy of publication. I acknowledge that I lack motivation, and I've blamed it on everything from my erratic schedule to this spirit-sucking winter. But Chicago's harshest has begun to lift, and even my most convincing excuses have begun to wear thin.

Partly I think I'm overwhelmed by where to start. Partly I believe that the lack of a deadline (like I had when I was in school) has kept me from putting any of my work out there. And it exists—I have plenty of material, mostly literary nonfiction, that I produced while in the writing program. Mostly, however, I think I'm afraid. Which is funny, because I've never failed at anything I've set out to do. Which is perhaps my problem—I've never set out to do anything I didn't already know I'd be successful at. I did well in school, and the writing program was no exception. My professors in large part lauded my work, even where I doubted myself. (For the record, I'm not convinced that I'm that good at this, but I think I'm at least good enough to get a job doing it. I think.)

In the next six months, my boyfriend and I will likely relocate from Chicago, thus forcing me to seek new work. I fear that I will settle back into a fitness job, where I know I'll do well, and that writing will continue to be a fantasy. Is there any hope for me? How can I give myself the kick in the ass that I so desperately need?

*Writing Only in My Dreams ...*

## Dear Dream Writer,

THE CONNECTION BETWEEN writing ... and writing for money or writing for success has to be broken. You need a good, strong, regular writing practice. The ego has to be broken for the voice to come through. The voice is what you want. The voice that makes no sense at first is what you want. The voice that sounds a little crazy is what you want. Try it.

You have to break the connection between ego and practice. The practice is the thing. How can you do that? You find a model in your life. What activities do you now practice for their own sake? Let's get very basic. What are your needs? You eat, you have sex, you listen to music, you exercise. What do you do for enjoyment alone? How do you manage your "inner life"? Do you meditate or practice any sort of religion? Do you enjoy cooking? Find a place like that in your life for your writing. You might try one of those books, too, like *The Artist's Way*. I don't know, I haven't read all those books but I have read some of them. *Bird by Bird* helped a lot.

Regardless of whether you sell your writing, you do it. Regardless of anything, you do it. It has to be a practice. There are many ways to get there. One way, which I have only come to very late in my career, is to be in a workshop. You probably had

> The ego has to be broken for the voice to come through.

those in college. Maybe you're sick of them. I was sick of them after college. But now the workshop is helping me. I am in such a workshop, but I am such an egotist and such a control freak that for me to be in a workshop I had to run my own. So be it. So I run my own. I walk around like I thought the whole thing up myself, but actually it is the Amherst Writers and Artists model. There are many models. This one works for me. I learn a great deal. And I am comforted. I need to be comforted because I am uncomfortable; I am a harsh self-critic. Others are not so lucky. I often hate my work. I simply detest it. I want to burn it. I think that it shows me in the worst possible light, as a whining, mewling infant, an idiot, a selfish prick. Yes, I am full of the most detestable self-hatred. And I am utterly transparent. This I take to be part of the job. Others do not. Others more successful have exquisite control; they write and do not feel the need to confess. What of it? Being a writer is permission to be disreputable: That is my chosen tradition. I am, shall we say, privately disreputable; I have my little jokes on the world and on myself; there is a dark side you don't see but you may feel it.

So give your self permission. Give your self permission to be wholly reprehensible. This is what they call the dark side. The dark side is where images arise unbidden before the ideas and the words. There is something there when you are not doing what you are supposed to do. So give yourself permission to be reprehensible because that is what is interesting and writing is not good or bad but only interesting. It lets us look through the peephole. Let yourself be a bad exercise person. Allow your vices. Give your vices voices. Let the voyeurs read you. Give people something to see. Give them a peep show. Take your clothes off in your writing because you'll be arrested if you take your clothes off in public but you can do it in your writing and you will not be arrested but you will be read. Be a bad person in your writing. The writing cleanses you. Be a bad person in your writing and then make yourself better and you have a changed character in a novel. It might be that simple: Start out bad and become good: That's change. Make a character do that. That's a character. Maybe we would call it drama or art. Anyway it helps you get on with the day.

Do it for these reasons. Keep doing it for these reasons. Do it for no reason. Keep doing it for no reason. When you are doing it because it is your voice, then it will not matter who is publishing you. It will have become apparent that writing is your friend. It will be what you would do in prison if they locked you up. It keeps you sane. It saves you. That's what it's for. Doing it for others sucks us dry. We have to do it for ourselves, for the love of it, for it. We have to give ourselves over to it like giving ourselves over to a lover or to the water, like giving ourselves over to the waves and sinking under. We just give ourselves to it. We surrender to it. We don't worry about who will publish it. We do it because we need to.

# I'm an artist terrified of
## the vast, blank canvas

*I know I have talent but I'm afraid to paint.*

Dear Cary,

I GRADUATED FROM high school nine years ago, and kind of just drifted aimlessly out into the world. For my entire life, art and English (particularly art) have been my great strengths and loves. I've been drawing since I was 3, painting since early high school, and reading voraciously and attempting new novels at least once a year all throughout.

So it seems logical that one of those subjects would be my chosen major for college. I always assumed I'd be an art major. I won awards in high school, even though I didn't really understand the significance of such a thing, and was accepted to special programs. In fact, I was so immersed in art that I let all other classes fall by the wayside and left myself with a GPA that would require me to attend a junior college before transferring to a university. Then, after I graduated high school, something funny happened. I had to work right away in order to get a car, so that I could drive to school, and somewhere in there I became so interested in so many things that I kind of just lost my sense of direction.

Over the years I have continued to paint on my own, although I have not been incredibly prolific, all the while intending to return to school. Finally, two years ago I returned to junior college and embarked on a course of study that I intended to have prepare me for a major in biopsychology, which is an incredibly rigorous major. I'm not even sure what drew me to this major, other than that I have a great amount of interest in how the brain works in response to mental illness, as my mother is schizophrenic. So, for the past two years I've been telling myself that I was going to go on and work in this field, probably teach it at a university, and maybe do some research. Everyone who sees my artwork asks me if I plan on doing something with it, and encourages me to do so, but I always brushed it off, despite the fact that if I could, I would drop everything else and paint for a living.

The past year or so I've been creating a little more often, and my skill has grown exponentially; it's like suddenly after years of stagnation I feel so natural in front of the canvas. My general sense of color and my actual technique have both grown by leaps and bounds, and more and more I have felt the tug to work creatively. It's like I'm seeing the world again the way I used to, everything is something that I can use on canvas as a part of my expression. This sounds like a great thing, and it is, but it is also the reason I need advice.

I was sitting in front of the canvas working the other day and it occurred to me that the entire reason I have not considered an art major as a real possibility since high school is that I am afraid to do so. I mean, one of my major goals has been to teach at a university, and obviously I could do that as either an art teacher or a biopsychology teacher. I think that I have been afraid that if I choose art as a major, that I will fail, I will have wasted my money on a major/degree that won't get me anywhere. I just don't know what to do. Should I take the risk and declare myself an art major and just go for it? Or should I declare another major that, although I find really interesting, is not one of my strengths?

*Aimless Artist*

Dear Aimless Artist,

YOU WERE SITTING in front of the canvas and realized you were afraid.

You figured it was fear of failure. But I don't think so. I think it was fear of discovery.

When an artist sits before a blank canvas frozen with fear it is because the subject is too terrifying to admit to consciousness. It is no mystery; rather, it is a truth that cannot be easily contained, that threatens to break one down. So one tries to hold it at bay. Thus you sit, immobilized, holding back the truth.

I think that truth is what you went through as a child, your story of growing up with a schizophrenic mother, how it affected your personality and your outlook on the world. I think that you are afraid to become a painter because if you become a painter you will have to discover the truth of your past. You will have to paint your mother.

It is good to do the things that terrify us the most.

So have her sit for you. Painting your mother will force you to regard her serenely, to study her features carefully and at length.

You can fix your mother—on the canvas.

You will learn to see her as she is: her dimensions, her color, her symmetry, her expressions. To paint her accurately you will have to look at her for a long time. In doing so, you may experience feelings that had been buried or frozen. That will be good. You may find yourself weeping as you paint. That will be good. You may hear the sound of icebergs falling into the sea. That will be good. It will be good to feel these things that you have held at bay for so long, and to feel them as a man now, not as a child, as a man capable of containing them and shaping them with your talent.

I suspect that one reason you are drawn to biopsychology is that you have a desire to fix your mother. But there is another way you can fix her. You can fix her on the canvas. Painting is your strength. That is what you need to use to fix your mother.

I know this is all a bit much. But I too wandered aimlessly after high school, and I too am a sensitive person who grew up in some degree of chaos and later had trouble learning to form coherent plans and carry them out.

I think I have something in common with you. I do not mean to frighten you. But I do mean to push you. I think you need to be pushed, as I at times have needed to be pushed. I think you need to spend some time feeling the way you were affected. You need to face this fact: You were raised by a woman who was mentally ill. Her behavior shaped you in unalterable ways. It hurt you but as compensation it also pushed you toward beauty. It is your calling to unearth and portray the way that she affected you. You have been shirking that calling. It is a painful calling and naturally we try to avoid painful things. That is what all the wandering was about. But you could wander forever and this truth would continue calling to you. It is the thing you need to deal with, the dragon you need to slay.

It is your calling, your truth: how it felt to have a mother whose world was a shattered vessel.

# Go away, can't you see I'm writing?!

*I'm finally starting to create again,*
*but people won't leave me alone!*


**Dear Cary,**

I'M A WRITER who's recovering from a serious case of burnout, exhaustion, writer's block ... whatever it was, it dried me up for over a decade. I wrote a lot when I was younger—poetry, short stories, half-completed novels—but it fell to a trickle by the time I was 30. My career kicked into gear (I'm a professional/technical writer) and satisfied some of my itch for writing. I got married and had children. We bought an older house that needed work. I became heavily involved with my professional society. Various other family responsibilities took up a lot of time and energy, too. All this time, people kept telling me that I should write because my earlier work had been promising. But I had nothing to write about. My ideas were fragmented, clichéd, or utterly trivial. The very act of writing was a chore. Even my work-related writing, which hitherto had been pretty interesting, degenerated into a dull routine of churning out the same things over and over and over again. I was relieved when my job was eventually shipped to India and I was laid off. Recently, though, I've snapped out of this funk. The layoff gave me a chance to breathe and get my bearings. I found a new job that pays somewhat less but is far more interesting than the previous one, my kids are a bit older and don't require as much hands-on supervision, we've been hiring contractors for the house instead of trying to do everything ourselves, and I have cut way back on the professional society. And I've started writing again! Currently I'm working on a fantasy novel that sprung semi-complete into my head. Writing it is a blast. It's kind of melodramatic and will probably never see the light of day, but I don't care. By finishing it, I'll gain the discipline to carry a book-length story through to the end. My hope is that it will break my writing logjam and lead to other things. So I'm just going with the flow to see where it takes me. What's the problem? Nobody will let me alone to write! Everyone in my family is curious about what I'm writing, but I really don't want to show it to anyone—especially as a work in progress. I've always viewed my fiction and poetry as my own private business and never wanted anyone else to read it until I was happy with it. (For some reason, though, it doesn't bother me to have drafts of my work writing reviewed by other people.) I don't want anyone reading over my shoulder as I type and offering unsolicited helpful advice. My spouse does this sort of thing all the time and I just don't want to deal with it. I need the freedom to screw up—and fix it—in peace! How else can I get back into the fiction-writing game? I try to write for an hour or so every day. I work on my laptop in the extra bedroom or the game room, but the kids find me and want to know what I'm doing. Most of the time I just wait until they're in bed, but then my spouse tracks me down and it starts again.

Until now, I've been putting them off. But then I start feeling guilty about not paying enough attention to my family, or letting the laundry pile up, or blowing off some other urgent thing that isn't getting done. And then my inner editor (who ordinarily is very helpful with my work writing) starts jabbing me with its red pen and telling me that I should be writing something significant. I had to beat it on the head with a typewriter to get it to shut up and let me start working on my story in the first place! Or I watch an "America's Most Wanted" episode about a woman who's so convinced that her husband is holding her back from greatness as a screenplay writer that she kidnaps their children and goes on the run, and I wonder if I'll end up like that. How should I handle this? I don't think I'm being neglectful or delusional. I just need some space to write in peace.

*Not Quite Virginia Woolf*

## Dear Not Quite Virginia,

IN *A ROOM OF ONE'S OWN*, Virginia Woolf says, "A woman must have money and a room of her own if she is to write fiction."

I agree with Virginia Woolf: I think you need money and a room of your own. I mean that literally.

You also need a community.

So I recommend that you find a writing workshop and attend it regularly for at least one year. Ideally, it would be a group that follows the Amherst Writers and Artists method, but just make sure there is a method. If there is no suitable workshop in your area, then buy the book *Writing Alone and With Others,* follow the detailed instructions in it and create your own workshop. That is what I did.

If the workshop is three hours long and you attend it once a week for a year, with possible breaks for vacation, that will give you, in one year, between 120 and 150 hours of writing time, thinking time, listening time, immersion in writing, your writing and the writing of others. Add to that your one hour a day of writing on your own, and that's at least 485 hours a year.

I went for many years believing that I did not need no stinking writers workshop. As a result of my upbringing and my reading and my education, I had come to believe, as implausible as this may sound, that my job was to become a writer like no other, a godlike, self-sufficient magician of words whose power could ward off the insults and predations of history, an autonomous hero, a superman, beyond human, motherless, beyond nurture, heedless of judgment, warmed by an eternal self-generating flame.

I think I was kinda wrong about that.

But that was my mistaken belief, my particular problem of male pride and intellectual doubt. Uncritical adherence to this notion had begun to cripple me creatively.

How did I come to believe that this was who a writer should be? Well, that is a whole story in itself, and perhaps to correct this legacy some man should write the equivalent of *A Room of One's Own*. Perhaps some man has. I wouldn't know. I've been too busy with my eternal self-generating flame and whatnot.

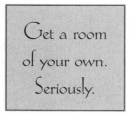

But anyway, this is the practical program I present to you: Get a room of your own and join a writers workshop. Think how much you can accomplish in 485 hours! It isn't just the work that gets done on the page that is beneficial, either. It is the consistent message that is sent to the heart or the unconscious, a message that says, "Writing is a good thing to do. Writing is a good thing to do. Writing is a good thing to do."

As to your domestic situation, well, the room of your own that you need may be outside your house. For that you need money. Virginia Woolf was talking about inherited money, or a windfall, but in your case wages will simply have to do. If you cannot keep your family out of the room that you write in, then you must find a room that your family does not go into. You can use your wages to find a room of your own in which to write. That is what you must do.

Citizens of the Dream:

Starting Over.
Starting a Band.
Just Not Giving Up.

# Is it too late to start a band at 45?

*I don't want to be a laughingstock, but I am a creative type!*

**Dear Cary,**

I AM IN a rather ridiculous dilemma that is driving me mad. I have never been very happy with my life. I have worked jobs, such as in retail, the restaurant industry and business offices, that have left me bored, unfulfilled and feeling like my soul has been crushed. On the side, I have done creative things: singing in bands, performing in local theater, putting together and performing with comedy troupes. These things kept me alive and interested in the world, but never paid the rent. I tried studying some of my creative interests in a university setting, but honestly don't feel I could be happy teaching. I've been told many times I have a near genius IQ and have always been an out-of-the-box thinker. The whole career track, partnering up with someone, buying a big house and driving an SUV thing makes me feel suicidal.

So my current dilemma? I am tired of being unhappy and not being myself. I work in "cubicle world," with dull-gray cubicles and nasty, mint-green walls. The people I work with, while nice, are not in any way relatable to me. I view them as mindless robots who do whatever society tells them to do. I feel as if I am quickly dying and soon to reach my breaking point.

The one thing in life I truly love is music, particularly industrial music. I listen to an industrial/goth radio station on the Net, and would love to start my own record label and also record my own album. The complication? In two weeks, I will be 45 years old. This is not some midlife crisis. I have always been an artistic, creative person and have always struggled to integrate this into the "real world." My therapist says go for it, the world is a different place now. But part of me always stops myself. I feel like I am too old and people will laugh me right out of town. I don't want to have only 20-something friends and be the laughingstock of the city. At the same time, I need a monetary source that brings me joy and a way to live out my quirky nature. So do I just go ahead and dive into the music scene, unafraid of being laughed at? Or should I accept that this ship has possibly sailed and find some other way to express myself?

*Lost in Portland*

## Dear Lost in Portland,

HOW DO YOU and I, with our myriad difficulties and lack of understanding, our lack of connections and affability, our inner machinery of self-defeat, how do we reconcile creativity with the practical requirements of living?

We start with ego deflation: The world doesn't owe us a living. Instead, we owe the world. We have been entrusted with something.

This is not easy. In certain ways, we are the worst of people. We do not make especially good members of the community. We spend our days messing with paint or digitizing sounds.

We create artistic business ventures and have difficulties with them. We pay insufficient attention to the matter of revenue. In short, we act as if the world owes us a living. We say, "Come out and support the arts!" And then we sit on a Tuesday night in an empty club feeling betrayed and confused.

But the whole premise was wrong from the start.

The debt is ours.

Of course, we can deny this debt. We can avoid the situation altogether. Many people do this—gifted with angelic voice or poetic storytelling ability or fine natural draftsmanship, they go into bond trading or auto repair. And why not? Nobody is offering them a job as a singer or storyteller or artist.

So welcome to the world. The world asks more of those to whom it has entrusted its gifts. It asks that we maintain a healthy standard of living plus devote many hours to music, practicing scales, and to art, drawing from life, working with color and meditating to keep the demons from revolt, and to writing nonsense that must be written, reading in search of wisdom or God, thinking, thinking, thinking—and sometimes to more and stranger things: sleeping a lot to find peace, going on retreat, flirting with madness.

It is our responsibility to ourselves and to the world to find ways to take care of ourselves, not to become a burden but to offer what we have. Toward that end, there is much to be said for scaling down our ambitions so that we can practice our art in a way that is regular and routine. We must work hard at it. We must work

> Your ego hunger is not your creative side.

steadily. But we must not expect to be rewarded overmuch for this, any more than someone who works for 40 years in insurance should expect to gain worldwide fame for structuring annuities in original and brilliant ways. We work quietly and steadily on our craft.

Consider this as well: We know how but we don't know how we know how. How do we know how to do what we do? How do we know what we know? We don't know. We don't know how we know.

The trapeze artist flies through the air and says, Like this! Do it like this!

But how ... how ... how? We can barely follow her movements with our eyes.

We don't know how we do it, so often we cannot teach it. All we can do is offer the structure in which others may learn; we can maintain the space in which the practice can be learned. We can sweep up after class and answer questions. We can say, Keep going! Keep going! Keep going! Do not be afraid!

So I don't know exactly what you ought to do. I think mainly your task is one of managing and distributing your creative endeavors, and also managing your money so that you can support these endeavors. In doing this, I suggest you try to separate your ego needs from your artistic needs. They are not the same thing. Your ego, starved as it is for support and encouragement, may well be the source of your grandiosity and hostility, the far poles of egomania and debasement between which the unmoored ego swings. So think of this, if you will: Your ego hunger is not your creative side. Your creative side is that which actually works—the joy you feel when listening, your actions, your performances, the things you actually create. If you are like me, you may often fantasize in impossible ways; perhaps you have fantasized since you were a young person that your creations will gain you worldwide adoration. I find myself—ashamed as I am to say it—fantasizing in this way. It has a childish quality to it, this fantasy. It feels like a narcissistic fantasy to some extent, the child imagining himself admired, like the baby Jesus, a hero born to a virgin.

This is crazy stuff, of course. That is the point. There is crazy stuff going on inside. But that is the deep structure speaking. And that deep structure is where we work. We try to create surfaces whose roots can be felt in that deep structure.

Have you ever seen kelp on the surface of the Pacific and marveled at how deep it goes, how far down in the dark, cold waters it is anchored on rocks and reefs and, who knows, sometimes on the hulks of shipwrecks? What we try to do is create surfaces that one feels are anchored deeply. You see the kelp bed, undulating in the waves, and you sense the depth of the water.

# Midlife crisis: I could have been a singer!

*I'm a mom with a 1-year-old and my life is passing before my eyes.*

**Dear Cary,**

MIDLIFE CRISIS!!!

OK, so I'm about to turn 38, and I think I'm having a midlife crisis. I've been married for almost three years (together for seven), and we have a beautiful 1-year-old son. The problem is this: I'm nowhere near where I thought I would be in my life. I have a decent career doing work for the public good, but I haven't done many of the things I had hoped to do when I was younger and now it's hitting me that I'm probably too old to pursue those dreams. I'm stuck in a small town, married to a man who has no ambition beyond making sure he TiVos the latest reality show, and I'm itching to just run away.

I won't do that, of course. I have an almost obsessive sense of duty.

Still, I need to find out what I'm still worth. My youth has trickled away and I'm feeling trapped and helpless. My dream life of pursuing a singing career is nothing but a faded memory now.

Is my life over? Is there any hope that I can someday break out of this small-town, debt-ridden, ho-hum life of mine without hurting the ones I love in order to do what I love? Or will I just wile away the rest of my life thinking "shoulda-coulda-woulda"?

Help!

*Coulda Been a Singa*

## Dear Coulda Been a Singa,

HERE ARE FOUR questions for you to answer:

When? When are you going to sing?

Where? Where are you going to sing?

What? What songs are you going to sing?

With whom? With whom are you going to sing?

Write those questions down and stare at them as if they were demons that you are going to light on fire with your eyes. Or alternatively stare at them as if they were deep questions whose answers will open the secrets of the universe.

Try answering one. Answer the "where" one. Do you have a place where you can sing or do you have to find one? Can you sing in the woods? Can you sing in the house? Can you sing in the studio of a singing teacher? Can you sing in the rehearsal hall of a band? Can you sing in church? Can you sing in your car? Pick a place where you are going to sing. Pick a place that feels right to you, where you will not look over your shoulder.

Then answer another one. Answer the "when" one. Do you have any time? With a 1-year-old, how do you get time? Do you steal time from your kid, is that how it feels? Well, maybe you need to make a withdrawal of some time, a small amount, for your singing. How much time can you withdraw? Can you get an hour? Can you get half an hour? How long can you sing before you are tired?

Then the "what." Pick a song to sing from beginning to end.

And then the "with whom." If you find the place, the time and the song, you can sing it alone, or you can sing it with someone. Or you can just write "alone" in that section for now.

So then:

Start singing.

If you contemplate the difficulties before you start singing, the difficulties may win. So do not recount the difficulties before you start singing.

But it is important to be real here. So let us recount the difficulties, numerous and legion:

To have a band is hard. To play shows is hard. To show up on time is hard. To rehearse is hard. To get along is hard. To hear is hard. To demonstrate parts is hard. To play in tune is hard. To fix the hard parts is hard. To make the hard parts sound easy is hard. To get the guitar player to change keys is hard. To communicate with the drummer is hard. To see yourself as others see you is  hard. To absorb criticism with equanimity is hard. To keep working to improve is hard.

What is not hard?

It is all hard.

So mostly we don't bother. But then awful thoughts of waste come into your head. The thoughts of waste hurt.

So you sing.

It is necessary to sing. It is necessary because you can't go around whining.

Have you got a calendar to write things in? You can get one at Office Depot. I got mine on sale because it was already April. So Lord knows I am no shining example. How long did I walk around saying I was going to start playing the guitar again one day? Was it how many years? How much of a whiner am I? How much do I procrastinate? How deep is the ocean? How high is the sky?

It is hard to devote many hours a week to playing music and attending to the incidental business and networking tasks involved in promoting a musical career and also meet your other social, psychological and economic needs. It is hard to live a day life in which you work for a company and a night life in which you rehearse, perform, write and socialize (or "network").

As you struggle to do these things, your heart may decide it wants a kitchen window and a kid or two. Your heart may decide it wants certain things that are not cool.

The price we pay for ignoring the heart is high.

So sweetheart, in a nutshell, just sing. Pick a time, a place, a song and, if necessary, a person. Write it in your little calendar.

I like this bit from the Alcoholics Anonymous "Big Book": "We will not regret the past nor wish to shut the door on it. We will comprehend the word serenity and we will know peace."

It implies arrival after long travel. It implies a stopping point. It implies, Give yourself a break.

There's nothing you can do about the past. But you can find some time to sing.

# At 56 I want an art history degree

*I hit the wall in my dead-end job, I'm sleeping on a friend's floor, but I have a dream!*

## Dear Cary:

I SUPPOSE YOU get this kind of letter often, but here goes: I am a 56-year-old guy who feels trapped in the workforce. After 30 years of working in the audiovisual/Web industry, I am frankly tired of it—it's gotten too technical and too software driven (which is not my strong suit). I want to start over, but because of some illness last year, I am unemployed and living on a very tolerant friend's floor. I'm getting some help from my brother, but it's barely enough to cover my basic expenses (car, phone, insurance, etc.). I am looking for a job in my field, but that seems to be going nowhere. I have come very close to committing suicide a couple of times in the past few months, and only some potential job offers (that in the end didn't pan out) have kept me on this side of the edge.

What I would really like to do is go back to school. I never graduated from college and have been winging it for over 35 years, playing the autodidact game and being very successful at it. I even wrote a book in the mid-1990s that I'm very proud of. But going back to school has challenges that are so large that I'm not even sure where to start. I do know that if I go back to school, it won't be for a "career." It's a little too late to start over as an architect or in another professional field. What I would really like to do is study art history and conservation—one of the few fields where it seems that age is an advantage. I've had a life-long interest in the field and have devoted most of my vacations to pursuing my appreciation of art and architecture. This is the first time in years that I've been excited by the thought of doing anything. But because of my financial situation it all seems like a huge wall that needs to be scaled. I'm at my wits' end and not sure where to start. I'm having problems sorting out my priorities. What do you think?

*Mike*


Dear Mike,

ACTUALLY, THIS SORT of letter does not come very often. So it is a pleasure to undertake an answer. Basically, I say go for it!

It's amazing what we can do when we can find the energy and organize our approach. I have no doubt that you could get a degree in art history and conservation. Besides, in the afterglow of the Fourth of July weekend, I'd say it's also the patriotic thing to do! This is the land of opportunity, is it not? So how would you begin? What would you do first?

This general overview may be a good place to start.

Then you might begin looking at specific programs.

Now, some people might say that before you start in on something like this, you ought to get the basics together first—find a job, place to live, etc. But I think it's the other way around. I think the way to get the basics together is to have a dream, a reason for living, a reason to get up in the morning. Without a dream to motivate you, it's going to be hard to deal with mundane issues. A dream can motivate you. It can also motivate people to help you. It can act as the vision toward which you move; if you have a big, motivating vision, it can dwarf the other problems in your life that might otherwise occupy all your time.

People might tell you to be sensible. But what is sensible about choosing a path that bores and depresses you? You are human.

You're not going to work hard at something you detest. You're not going to succeed at it. You're only going to succeed at something you are motivated to do. So not only is this the smart choice, it is, in a sense, your only choice.

Illness and job loss can undermine your confidence and self-worth. Having a goal that you believe in can act to restore that self-worth. So work on this dream. It will motivate you and it will motivate others. And it sells.

That is, you are going to need to sell yourself. It is easier to sell people on a big idea than a small idea. Say you went around to your friends, or you went to city agencies and the like, and said, "Hey, I'm a 56-year-old guy with no college degree and, uh, I got sick and hit a stretch of bad luck and lost my job, and I'm living on a friend's floor and I need help." That indicates that you need help but it does not contain a dream. It isn't motivating. It doesn't

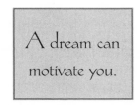

A dream can motivate you.

sell. But if you say, "Hey, I'm a guy who has taken some knocks but I've got a dream—I want to get a college degree in art history and conservation—and I know it's a little unusual but that's my dream and I'm going for it," then you are a story. Newspapers run stories about people with dreams, unusual people who have the courage to start fresh in life. It's something that makes us smile. So I suggest you concentrate on this and work toward it.

This is the kind of thing I'm thinking about. And this. Or how about "How I Got Into Law School at 47"? And here's somebody who went back to college late in life for a degree in art history.

So it can be done. You will need help. You will need emotional support and encouragement. You will feel some days that it's not worth it, or that it is impossible. You will need a nudge now and then to keep going. But you can do it. Stick with people who will encourage you and keep you moving.

It's going to take a lot of work, but if it's something worth working for, you will find the energy to do it.

I salute you! I wish you luck! Now get going!

# I'm a singer—but I drift from waitress job to waitress job

*I don't know how to settle down. But I'm almost 30 and don't want to waste my life!*

## Dear Cary,

I'VE WRITTEN TO so many advice columnists and no one ever answers. I am plagued by problems—for years. In general, what the hell is the deal with me? I was so blithe and great and happy in childhood—but ever since I was, oh, 15, things have gone downhill, and I'm just about 29 now. After high school, I moved away to go to college, but I quit after two years because I wasn't really happy. I wanted to be a singer, as I had since I was 5, and I was doing some singing. But in general I felt unhappy, there was something lacking, and also I was in a relationship I wanted to get away from. So I quit school and moved away. In my new location, I sang a bit, got into another relationship, really wanted to get out of it, and moved away again. In my new location, I sang more, met another man, moved away with him, definitely had to leave, and—yes, moved away again. That was when I moved back in with my parents. I waitressed, moved to a new place, waitressed and sang there, then decided to fin-ish school and did, but hated it the whole time. The school was lacking academically and was in a podunk town-—where I met a new man, moved in with him, and then, about a year later, yes, moved away. Now I am living with my parents again and feeling quite at a loss.

I always dreamed of great things in life. But I'm going to be 30 and I've done nothing—nothing to be able to say, "Hey, I've made it!" In short, I've made nothing for myself (except learning the hard way whom not to fall in love with). I'm waitressing again, and yes, singing (in a tiny show where I make $75 a week and wear a rubber cone head—don't ask). I think I'll stop moving—I've wanted to for years. (Though I will move out of my parents' house.) But just what the hell should I do? I've moved around since childhood—four years is the longest I've ever lived anywhere, and one year is the longest I've ever held a job. There are so many things I am interested in—writing, editing, singing, dancing—but career-wise, my résumé is just a long list of waitressing and oddities. Where I am now is the closest thing I have to a childhood home, and I have family here (my parents only live here half the year), and so I feel I might stick here. So sometimes I think I am finally ready to do "my life" and make something out of it, besides a mess. But other times I am very scared to think of the future—I don't want to be forever drifting. I want a fulfilling career, a husband and family. But how to start? What am I to do? I am so bored waitressing and I have about three friends spread over the U.S. due to me being neither here nor there but always taken up with a tumultuous relationship with a man. Tell me—where shall I start and while I'm waiting for roots to grow, how can I not be so bored?

*Chronically Waiting, Dreaming and Scheming for a Life That Is Passing Me By*

P.S. I have thought about performing musicals on a cruise ship but I need to build something for the future, not just another temporary excitement!

## Dear Chronically Waiting,

SO YOU'VE WRITTEN to lots of advice columnists and nobody ever writes back? Well, I'll write back. I'll write back because there are certain things you need to know that no one tells you, things I have learned the hard way, things that are simple but can take a lifetime. You don't have a lifetime.

So here is the deal in a nutshell: Your actions have put you in the spot you're in. I'm not blaming you. I'm just directing your attention to the correct area. It's time to change your actions. How do you do that? You adopt a different set of criteria for making decisions.

You left college after two years because you weren't happy. "Happy" was a criterion for leaving college. That will have to change. "Happy" is not a criterion anymore. "Required for the next step" is your new criterion.

For the next five years I suggest you do only those things that are required to take you to the next step. It will be hard to change but it is doable and simple and it will give you a much better shot at being happy.

Where do you start? You start by clarifying the goal toward which you are going to struggle for the next five years. I suggest creating a goal that is obtainable through hard work and that is measurable. I would say your goal right now should be to attain proficiency and excellence in your craft.

You may want to be a star. You may think that should be your goal. But I don't think so. I think your goal should be to attain proficiency and excellence in your craft. The desire to be a star may be a vision that motivates you. You may benefit from visualizing yourself as a star. But for a goal you need something that is under your control. Proficiency and excellence in your craft is something you can actually attain. It may sometimes precede stardom, but it is never a guarantee of stardom. There is no guarantee of stardom. But there are guaranteed milestones of proficiency and excellence that are obtainable.

So let's say that your No. 1 goal in life is now to attain proficiency and excellence in your craft of singing and acting. That's very simple. How is that done? It's done through education and hard work.

If you adopt this one goal, your decisions can all flow from this one premise: Your purpose is to attain proficiency and excellence in your craft. What do you do? Whatever you have to do in order to attain proficiency and excellence in your craft, that's what you do.

How? You take voice lessons and acting lessons. You build your network of fellow singers and actors. You locate yourself in the best place possible for getting that kind of education, experience and contacts.

What place is that?

Well, there's no doubt that Los Angeles and New York are the best places to go if you already have the skills. But where are the best places to learn these skills? Not necessarily Los Angeles and New York.

Take a look at the latest U.S. News and World Report rankings of top national universities for voice and opera majors. Also see the magazine's rankings of schools for acting majors.

I'm not saying categorically that you should go back to school for a B.A. in performance. But I'm saying

> It's not about happy. It's about what is the next step?

you want to gain the hard facts and take concrete actions. Maybe you look and find the best teacher and that teacher is in one of these towns with a top-rated drama and voice program. The talent tends to cluster. So you might move to a town with one of the top-rated schools. It's this kind of thinking that I'm suggesting.

You may find it impossible to sit long enough and concentrate long enough to make the right plans. There may be more work involved in doing this. Some of this work may involve understanding what happened when you were 15. You were happy and then something happened. Sometimes things happen in adolescence and we form patterns of behavior as a result and we don't find out until years later how that happened. We underestimate the power of these events somehow; we believe that we are able to make the right decisions but those decisions keep putting us in a bad spot. So in order to make this orderly shift, you may have to enlist the help of others. That would make sense.

Want to know a secret? I can hardly do anything on my own. Actually, I now have three professionals helping me cope with life. Three! One of these people is paid for by the city, as one of its programs to help small businesses. One is paid by my health insurance through my employer. And one of them I pay out of my pocket. OK, I'm kind of a basket case, but I'm just saying, there's nothing wrong with going out into the world and asking for help. It's all worth it.

Want to know another secret? I want to be a singer, too. I used to be in a punk/new wave band. You want to hear me sing a punk song? I'm pretty bad! Tell you what. If you will promise me that you will go and start working seriously on your craft, I will send you—no, better yet, I will place on the Web for all to hear—a song that I wrote and sang in the early 1980s and, well, OK, that's just the deal I'm offering. Because you need some kind of "accountability buddy." You need somebody to be accountable to who won't let you slide.

So you write to me and let me know what you're doing, and then I will do this. I will place myself on the line, so that we have some accountability, you and me. So we have a deal.

I'm almost at my deadline now so I have to wrap up. But I want to say that the beauty of changing your life in this way, wrapping it around a purpose, is that your life begins to have a demonstrable shape. Someone asks, well, what brings you to Evanston, Ill.? And you say, well, I'm trying to become the best singer I can possibly be, and they have the best teachers here.

Having a goal makes your life a story. What is a story? It's somebody who wants something and tries to get it. It's what the person wanted and how he or she went about trying to get it. So you make your life a story. Then everything falls into place.

It's not as easy as it looks. It's not easy to change your life. It's not easy to do things differently. But it can be done.

# Should I give up on having a life in the theater?

*I've let go of my acting career, but it won't let go of me.*

Dear Cary,

I'VE COMPOSED THE same letter many times over the past year without ever having hit the Send button because, during a writing episode, sooner or later I've been able to bury my little problem in my head just long enough to keep it from going nuclear. But this morning. Oh Jesus. One little phone call, and my emotions are stealthily clawing their way up through the grave. Again. Oh, the drama.

I never explicitly grew up with the need to become an actress—it was never a life's goal—but nevertheless I graduated with a degree in theater (I had fallen in love with Shakespeare) and went on to audition for, be accepted in, and finish an MFA professional actor training program out West. I moved to New York like aspiring actors are supposed to do, got tired of temp jobs and being lonely and broke and living off of friends and not having an agent. I left after only five months to take advantage of another job opportunity in another state—in a different field 180 degrees away from theater.

Wouldn't you know it, that opportunity fell through, and since I had spent all of my money on the move, I found myself once again broke and stuck and lonely—in New England.

I've been in Boston for four and a half years. The city is OK; wherever you go, there you are, right? I've stayed at one crappy job only to move on to another crappy job because I can't figure out what I want. Ironically, whenever I have made the decision to want something, I have always gotten it. Always. I want to want something again. Even if I'm wrong! I'm so sick of being in limbo.

So here's what prompted me to hit the Send button: I went to a play last night, something I rarely do nowadays because it's a surefire way to unleash old demons. The theater is incredibly seductive—or at least my memories of it are. Now I've been thinking nonstop about the creative life vs. the present-day office life that I hate, and the breezy ways of actors vs. the uptight lawyers in their suits who occupy my building. I'm in my mid-30s now, and for the last two years I've been working as the assistant to a very needy octogenarian real estate entrepreneur (and I have little patience with needy men). This is the last place I expected to be.

I know I'm romanticizing a lot of this, because I never did honestly see myself living the New York actor's life in the first place, but I spent so much time—a good 10 years—in some kind of world of theater, be it either educational or, through my graduate school MFA program, professional, that I can't help feeling confused about where I think I want to belong. I know I don't feel like myself in an office.

So here's the rub. Myself and members of my MFA class all became Equity eligible after graduation (basically means that we are free to join Actor's Equity, the professional actor's union). I was disillusioned at the time and put off joining. I never joined. But seeing that play last night made me mildly curious, so I called Equity this morning to check on my eligibility standing.

Guess what. Seems I'm no longer eligible. My beginning date of eligibility was Oct. 27, 2000. Actors have five years from that date to join Equity after becoming eligible. I've expired! Grad school was a stupid waste of time and money. I'm an idiot.

This seems like the perfect opportunity to let go of a dream that never really was. Even though I detest my job, I have a lot of other things going for me—I'm in a great relationship, I'm healthy, I'm still active and curious about life—but even though I have done nothing during the last four and a half years to perpetuate the need of keeping a theater dream alive, still I keep it alive. I want it dead. I want to move on. But I still feel a part of me—even though it's a constantly diminishing part of me—is there (like I said, theater is seductive). If I could only figure out something else to want, I would be OK. But I feel like this stupid theater thing is what's keeping me from moving on and wanting something else.

So how do I let it go? And how do I get out of my own way? I hope you can help me.

*A Reluctant Drama Queen*

## Dear Reluctant Drama Queen,

IN THE SAME way that you penned many letters before finally sending one to me, I have written many words to you already, before realizing that they were all rather empty. Perhaps because your question hits so close to home, because it is a question that I struggle with daily, I have been writing around it for the past two days.

So I had to go back to the beginning this morning and start again, trying to talk to you in a calm, level voice, aware that my motives are not pure, that I am stirred up and conflicted (I would like to impress you; I would like to dazzle you; I would like to show you that I know you; and all the while I am playing to the audience, not to you). But ... I do this a lot, don't I?—I write draft after draft, unsuccessfully, before coming to, as it were, to find you still sitting there waiting to hear something useful that is not about me. And still, even as you are clutching your bag readying to go—still I insist that I must carefully recap for you all the fruitless byways I have already explored; while much of my trouble is simply procedural and not artistic at all, still I allude to the difficulty of my craft, looking for sympathy, which is so co-dependent and unprofessional!

But as I fumble around like Columbo, I take in more than I seem to. I have an idea about you, about who you are and what your real problem is. To be blunt, I think it's clear that you have to find a place in your life for theater work. This may mean making some adjustments. If you cannot make a decent living working only in the theater, then you must work two jobs.

Doing this may involve making some discoveries about your capacities, your temperament. It may mean learning to live with

Stop running from what you need.

some psychic discomfort. But I say this because I sense that you and I are close in temperament. The way you have scaled remarkable heights only to find yourself shrunken into servitude—this I recognize, this outsize capacity for expansion and contraction and for extravagant achievement and careless waste, the feeling that one's calling is not a gift but a burden, the desire to be done with it once and for all—all these things I recognize.

In fact—and here I will share with you a paragraph drafted earlier—I too let my eligibility for a professional milestone lapse. I completed all my coursework, passed my orals and had my creative thesis approved in graduate school for a master's degree in creative writing. Then I delayed for seven years the completion of some minor paperwork. Now I cannot have that master's degree that I worked so hard and so proudly to obtain. Strange, is it not? Indeed, such perverse delay is in one way a kind of proud renunciation, a protest. At bottom there is something pure and revolutionary about it. But there is also something self-destructive. The two work together in tandem, in a death dance, the revolutionary and the suicidal.

To be neither revolutionary nor suicidal but to pursue our work as it is revealed to us, to do the tasks that are handed to us by the force of our nature: That is the struggle that we actually must undertake to be whole.

You have a keen desire to work in the theater. This is the work that is handed to you by the force of your nature. Yet you run from it. Running from it pains you. Yet still you run. You will have to stop running sometime and face it.

We do not always find the work we think we will find; it is sometimes more as if the work finds us when we are ready. Look at me, writing an advice column. What am I to make of this? It is not drama or poetry or fiction or song. What is it? Why am I doing it? Why am I not onstage at some glittering event with some other writers whom I openly admire but secretly deride, all the while knowing nothing of their work? Why do I recoil from events at which writers are present? There I am, the untidy man in the corner at the art opening, drinking from the can in a paper bag! Why?

Well, perhaps because you and I want far more from the world than we let on. We have extravagant gifts, but we are deeply flawed. We are children! We don't know how to act! We can't concentrate! We grow bored and impatient! We'd rather slave away in an office than do mediocre art ... and all the while, we lie helpless before the gods; no matter what, we cannot stop doing what we do. We are in fact led to accomplish much, even as we deny what we are doing. At least you got the MFA. I didn't even get the degree. I started a punk band. What was that all about?

Anyway, now that I'm leveling with you, here is the way I was going to begin my response; here is my cerebral summation of the situation:

I see you onstage in a play. In the play something is hidden.

What is hidden is your essential nature. It cannot be killed. It won't go away. It must be dealt with.

What is the classic dramatic resolution to the problem of our struggle against our essential nature? Either this: We fail tragically fighting it; we go mad; we become rigid and monomaniacal; we shut ourselves into a room; we try to kill everything that disagrees with or threatens us. Or this: We make a discovery; a miracle occurs; the thing that threatened us is transformed, through revelatory action, into something beautiful that sustains us. Dammit, I am an actress! Dammit, let's put on a show!

Sure, make fun of it. But it's the truth.

That's what I had written. Isn't that rather stilted and pretentious? Sure, there is probably some truth in it. But Oh, the cleverness of placing you, an actress, onstage in order to make some point about "classic dramatic resolution"!

Here, though, is something else that perhaps we share: the grandiosity of our expectations. Have you ever felt, for instance, that if you are really to do theater that it must be the most pure, the most white-hot, the most completely absorbed thing imaginable—that if you are to do it, you must surrender to it so completely that you might in fact disappear, or die, or become someone else, or stand naked and sobbing in the footlights? Is there an apocalyptic expectation deep in your heart, or a feeling that if you are to become an actress then you will be an actress like no other ... is there a fear that to acknowledge this dream means to expose something, or risk failure, or turning out to be ordinary?

I can only speak for myself in this regard. (Oh, boy. That's probably just pitiful me we're talking about.) I know that for myself the dream is to be an artist, but that attempting to live as an artist, the poverty, the betrayals, the insecurity ... have all led me to turn away, to seek jobs in journalism and industry. But I continue, in my way. I continue working. I know that I lack certain essential abilities. I am trying to acquire them. It seems to me that I have no choice.

Well, I have tried to give you some of my thoughts. I could suggest other things as well—that your impulsiveness may be harming your chances of gaining a career, that you may need to learn to tough it out in a bad job while you keep going on auditions, that you may have a low threshold of psychic pain, that you need to simply work within your limits, things like that. But the one thing I would like to say most plainly is this: I do not think you can successfully fight your essential nature; if you fight it you only go mad; it must be transformed through revelatory action into something that sustains you.